Thank you for your
interest and support.

Lesly.

When a Hostel Becomes a Home:
Experiences of Women

When A Hostel Becomes A Home: Experiences of Women

Lesley D. Harman
Department of Sociology
King's College
The University of Western Ontario

Garamond Press
Toronto, Ontario

A publication of Garamond Press.

Garamond Press
67A Portland Street
Toronto, Ontario M5V 2M9

Printed and bound in Canada.
Typeset at PageCraft in Halifax.

Harman, Lesley D.,
        When a Hostel Becomes a Home

1st ed.
Bibliography: page 109
Includes indexes.

ISBN 0-920059-80-5

Canadian Cataloguing in Publication Data

Harman, Lesley D.
   When a hostel becomes a home

(Network basics series)
Bibliography: p.
ISBN 0-920059-80-5

1. Homeless women. 2. Homeless women – Services for.
3. Women's shelters. I. Title. II. Series.

HV1444.H37 1989   362.8'39   C89-094304-4

To Thelma McCormack:

teacher, mentor, friend.

In my mother's day, a woman's biggest fear was that she might one day become a cleaning lady. Today, a woman's biggest fear is that she might one day become a bag lady.

—Joy Reid

It seems that Man Alone is a figure of profound, tragic and noble philosophical significance, while woman alone is a welfare problem.

—Mary O'Brien

We're talkin' survival here.

—"Lisa"

Contents

Preface 9

CHAPTER ONE
The Creation of the Homeless Woman: The Myth of Home 13
    Typification, Domestication and the Urban Ground Rule 13
    The Creation of the "Homeless Woman" 15
    Of No Fixed Address: Housing as Social Control 21
    Visible vs. Invisible Homelessness 22
    The Myth of Home 24

CHAPTER TWO
Patriarchy and Social Policy: Hostels for Homeless Women 28
    Patriarchy, the State, and Social Policy 28

CHAPTER THREE
Becoming a Volunteer:
An Ethnographic Approach to Studying Homeless Women 35
    Choosing a Method 35
    Choosing a Hostel 39
    Becoming a Volunteer 40

CHAPTER FOUR
The Hostel as Reproducing Domesticity:
Structure and Organization 45
    The Structure of the Hostel 45
        1. Intake 45
        2. Boarding Arrangements 46
        3. House Rules 47
        4. Lock-up Room 49
        5. Donations Room 50
        6. Sunday Dinners 50
    The Drop-In Centre 51
    The Housing Office 51
    Conclusion 52

CHAPTER FIVE
Staff, Power, and Relations of Control   55
   Relations between Staff and Residents   55
   A Dramaturgical Analysis   56
   An Effort to "Get More"   58
     1. Food   58
     2. Tokens   59
     3. Bingo Prizes   59
     4. Tobacco   61
     5. Desirable Clothing   63

CHAPTER SIX
Going Home for Sunday Dinner:
The Subculture of Homelessness   67
   Sunday Dinner at the Hostel   68
   The Kitchen   70
     1. Planning the menu and shopping   73
     2. Preparing food   75
     3. Setting the domestic stage   75
     4. "Managing" the performance   76
     5. Cleaning up the set   79
   Conclusion   80

CHAPTER SEVEN
"Here I am a Somebody": Residents' Experiences of Self   81
   Lisa   82
   Claudia   85
   Adrian   86
   April   87
   Rosemary   89
   Tamara   93
   Evelyn   95

CHAPTER EIGHT
When a Hostel Becomes a Home: The Cycle of Dependency   101
   Powerlessness   102
   Lack of Autonomy   102
   Replication of Domesticity   102
   Idolation of Female Beauty   102

Conclusions and Implications   103
   Homelessness as Deficiency   104
   Hostels as Reproducing Domesticity   105
   Alternative Helping Strategies   106

Bibliography   109

About the Author   114

Preface

It is hard to say at what point this project unfolded as first a possibility, and then an inevitability. Something important began while I was teaching a course in the sociology of deviance at York University, during the final year of my Ph.D. program. I was giving a lecture on homelessness and one student asked, "What's all this about 'bag ladies'? I've never seen one and I don't think we have any in Toronto." I suggested that the fact that she lived, worked, shopped and studied in North York might have something to do with her perceptions, and that she might have a change of heart if she ventured downtown. The next week she could hardly wait to announce to the class that she had "seen one," confirming that I was right and that "there really are such things as 'bag ladies'." My interest in the cultural production of homeless women grew, and came to encompass a concern for the experience of homelessness among this increasingly visible category of women. I applied for and was awarded a postdoctoral fellowship to study the experience of homelessness among women.

This book is the product of a participant observation study, conducted over 1983-84, of women who sought social assistance at three facilities for homeless women in an Ontario city: a hostel, a day-time drop-in centre, and a housing service. The study was terminated at the end of the first year of my fellowship because I had been offered a full-time teaching position in another city. While I regret that I was unable to continue in the field, I nevertheless feel compelled to share the insights gained during my study. As time has passed and as the issue of homelessness has become the focus of national and international concern, culminating in its recognition in the naming of 1987 as the International Year of the Homeless, I have come to believe that this book might contribute in some small way to our understanding of the politics and experiences of homelessness among women.

In putting forth my findings, I do not make claims as to their general application to all homeless women or to all of the services offered for them, nor do I attempt to provide answers to all of the questions that are currently being asked about homelessness. My aim is a relatively simple one: to tell a story about the women that I encountered, and to show how their lives became bound up with social services, and ultimately came to mirror the dominant patriarchal ideology governing "woman's place."

I will argue that the lives of homeless women and the types of social services offered for them can only be understood in the light of the larger context of patriarchy and social control within capitalist society. The very notion of "homelessness" among women cannot be invoked without noting the ideological climate in which this condition is framed as problematic, in which the deviant categories of "homeless woman" and "bag lady" are culturally produced. The particular human services that are provided cannot be critically evaluated without an eye to the underlying conception of "woman's place" and the conditions necessary to reproduce it. Finally, prospects for change cannot be outlined without attention to the larger human condition and the contemporary struggles which women face.

Chapter One, "The Creation of the Homeless Woman: The Myth of Home," introduces a critical context for understanding the production of the devalued category of "homeless woman," and opposes the attributed deficiency of "homelessness" against the mythologized norm of "homefulness." Chapter Two, "Patriarchy and Social Policy: Hostels for Homeless Women," examines how the prevailing myth of home governs designs for the delivery of human services for homeless women. Chapter Three, "Becoming a Volunteer: An Ethnographic Approach to Studying Homeless Women," explains the processes entailed in my moving toward and entering the world of the homeless. Chapter Four, "The Hostel as Reproducing Domesticity: Structure and Organization," describes the physical environment of the hostel and the system of rules and sanctions imposed. Chapter Five, "Staff, Power, and Relations of Control," reveals the political climate within the hostel and the polarization between residents and staff. Chapter Six, "Going Home for Sunday Dinners: The Subculture of Homelessness," provides a dramaturgical analysis of how the hostel-as-home is lived out on a weekly basis. Chapter Seven, "Here I Am a Somebody: Residents' Experience of Self," takes a closer look at the experiences of some of the women interviewed, and shows how the hostel came to take on the characteristics of home for many of the regular residents. The concluding chapter, "When a Hostel Becomes a Home: The Cycle of Dependency," provides a critical analysis of how the relations between the lived experiences of homeless women and the dominant ideology of patriarchy and capitalism serve the explicit goals of providing shelter while at the same time implicitly serving to reproduce domesticity by making homeless women once again "homeful" within a context of dependency.

I am grateful to the Social Sciences and Humanities Research Council of Canada for awarding me a postdoctoral fellowship and for the additional research grant (#410-83-1211) which helped to offset some of the expenses incurred during the study. I am also grateful to my colleagues at York University who encouraged me to pursue this project, particularly Thelma McCormack, Desmond Ellis, and Gottfried Paasche. It has taken some years for this work to finally appear in print, and my thinking has matured and taken shape through the many opportunities I have had to share my ideas with colleagues and students at Trent University, King's College, and The University of Western Ontario, and through correspondence with others who have read and reviewed my work. Salient among these are Norman Bell, Margrit Eichler, Gayle Hutchison, Marion Pirie, Jim Rinehart, Ted Schrecker, Bin-Ky Tan, and Candace West. Sandra Aylward, James Côté, Sandra Kirby, and Kathryn Kopinak kindly read the manuscript and provided helpful comments. Several members of the hostel staff read the manuscript in its final stages. They were able to suggest ways in which the hostel and social services in general have evolved since the study was conducted, information that has been incorporated where possible. Some also expressed different interpretations from those advanced in this book.

Most importantly, I would like to recognize the women who gave me a trust that is rare in the world of homelessness. Both the staff and the clients of the services I studied were honest, frank, and patient with me as I stumbled my way into their world. At the end of the day, this is their book. As interlocutor I only hope to have translated it faithfully.

Lesley D. Harman
March 1989

Chapter One

The Creation of the "Homeless Women": The Myth of Home[1]

In recent years, "homeless women" have become a visible and devalued category in North American cities. The "social problem" of homelessness has become real to sociologists, social workers, media, and public alike. Sociologists as well as common-sense members participate in the creation and perpetuation of social reality through the ongoing generation of social categories. These categories reflect ideological prescriptions of how "normal" individuals of a particular sex, class, age, and race should behave. The recent identification, recognition and treatment of "homeless women" lends itself to analysis from this perspective.

In this chapter, it will be argued that homeless women are perceived and treated as social deviants because they do not conform to prevailing norms regarding "woman's place"—norms that are both firmly rooted in and supportive of the dominant patriarchal and capitalistic social structure of North American society. In light of the hegemonic "myth of home," "homelessness" is defined as a deficiency, a condition to be remedied.

Typification, Domestication, and the Urban Ground Rule
The categories or typologies through which members of social groups define others as conforming or deviant are key tools in the social construction of social problems. Professionals in various diagnostic, helping, and social control occupations, or "imputational specialists" (Lofland, 1969), have the authority to impute deviant characteristics to individuals, and to legitimate certain types of treatment by the state. The defining power of imputational specialists is great indeed.

Whereas Lofland refers to professionals such as doctors, lawyers, psychiatrists, and social workers in their capacity as diagnosticians, it may also be useful to see that a critical public of "amateur sociologists" has evolved for whom such typification is an everyday sense-making activity. As Goffman demonstrates throughout most of his work (1959,

1961, 1963a, 1963b, 1971), urban actors engage in a practice of typifying others according to the minimal indicators that are present in the particular frame of any encounter. All members who are fluent in the language of presentation of self are imputed to intend that they be read in a particular way, and in turn read others accordingly. The conversation of symbols replaces the conversation of spoken language as the dominant mode of interaction in the city. Wright (1971) calls this practice the "urban ground rule":

> Urban people are quite sensitive to any behavioral cues which allow them to locate an individual categorically, whether that cue is overt behavior or some expressive symbol, such as clothes, property, or even bumper stickers. Indeed, it is virtually impossible to say or do anything in an urban setting without some categorical meaning being attached to it. And since categories tend to be equated with people, perhaps it is in this way that urban men come to consider what they do as being who they are. (320-1)

The urban ground rule is a kind of communication that allows strangers to coexist in urban society at a level of nonverbal "understanding." Knowing the language of membership enables one to operate on the basis of "trustworthy recipes" (Schutz, 1944) in the negotiation of everyday life. Within the trustworthy recipes of any population there is a tolerance for "normal" or "acceptable" deviance (Harman, 1985).

It is in encounters with anomalous situations that new categories arise. This is precisely the process employed by the information media in their search for "news," by social scientists in their attempts to "explain, predict, and control," and social policy makers in the targeting of populations in need of human services and in the distribution of those services: in the quest for "truth" and "justice," everything anomalous must be accounted for, given a name, given a place.

Todd Gitlin (1979) argues that the hegemonic processes of the mass media do not simply innocently reflect "objective reality" in the reporting of social problems. Rather, they exercise significant social control in the process of "domesticating" social problems (p. 262). "Domestication" entails a notion of *home*, and as a process implies the linguistic transformation of an entity from outside to home. This can be seen as a three-stage process in typification: (1) appropriation; (2) bringing home; and (3) control.

Domestication involves appropriation in the sense of owning and transforming. The home is traditionally the context for privacy and property. The maxim, "A man's home is his castle," reflects the long-standing priority given, in both common law and codified law, to the home as the "last outpost" of men against public justice. The difficulties in attempting to enforce the law against assault when it occurs within the context of the home—a problem which has enormous consequences in terms of the perpetuation of the "wife battering problem" (Cole, 1982; MacLeod, 1980, 1987; Thompson & Gilby, 1980)—is rooted in the long-standing perception of equivalence between "home," "privacy," and "property." This perception is maintained by public (including neighbours who "don't hear" the screaming), police (who have been generally reluctant to intervene in family violence), and judges (who have maintained that "keeping the family together" should be the goal of judicial intervention). Appropriation, in turn, implies an ongoing "bringing home" or privatization, where home provides a continuous relationship between past and future in the appropriation of the present. Finally, domestication results in a situation of control within the realm of the private and owned.

Domestication is a powerful and useful metaphor. To "domesticate" social problems is to come to control them in terms of the ongoing familiarity of a common-sense world. This familiarity is linguistically produced in the form of naming. Domestication therefore has implications for how we come to have the licence to typify. Linguistically, appropriation, bringing home, and control translate the new into the existing language which in turn serves to *familiarize the strange*, to make "normal" or "acceptable" that for which our present tools of typification will not suffice.

The social construction of social problems is a collective form of norm definition. If it is couched in language, then it is couched in the most universal tool of social control. To name, to create a typology, is to entrench an anomalous situation within the hegemonic language of membership of a community (Harman, 1987a). The naming of a problem, in turn, legitimizes further action which might be taken to "solve" the problem. In other words, the metaphor of domestication may be extended beyond the linguistic to apply to the physical application of appropriation, bringing home, and control of deviants in the form of social policy making and implementation, with perhaps the most blatant example being the domestication of "deviants" through total institutionalization (Goffman, 1961). The domestication of homeless women can be understood as a more subtle but no less real form of social control.

The Creation of the "Homeless Woman"

The process through which "homeless women" are identified as anomalous and typified as deviant cannot be understood without considering the culturally prescribed "normal" roles for women within patriarchal society. Patriarchy, or the structural arrangement of male dominance, is supported by a largely nonconscious ideology (Bem & Bem, 1983) and is perpetuated through an unequal role structure for men and women. The gendered division of labour in North American society has systematically assigned high-status paid labour to men, and low-status, unpaid domestic labour to women. This arrangement, although a *cultural* product, is so deeply entrenched in institutions, beliefs and practices as to have taken on the characteristics of being a product of *nature*. So, within the patriarchal structure it is not unusual for individuals to argue that woman's place is *naturally* in the home, and that any changes in these practices are *unnatural*.

Sociological thinking has not been immune to the influences of the patriarchal order, and in fact early conceptualizations of "the family" claimed that, because the nuclear family was organized along such lines, this must mean that the gendered division of labour was "functional" for the society. Such an ideal-typical family was conceptualized by Parsons and Bales (1955), for whom gender role typing on the basis of biologically-determined "functions" cast males and females in limited "instrumental" and "expressive" roles. The image is of the nuclear family as a functioning system based on roles of instrumental superior (father), expressive superior (mother), instrumental inferior (son) and expressive inferior (daughter). Patterns of behaviour associated with instrumentality include providing food, shelter, discipline, and control. Patterns associated with expressivity include providing affection, nurturance, warmth, and conciliation. There is a clear hierarchy attributed to the membership of the nuclear family such that father dominates the other members and mother is dependent upon father's dealings with the outside world in order to fulfil her function within the home.

Feminist theorists have been roundly critical of the functionalist view of the family. Weitz (1979) points out that this characterization of expressive-instrumental roles "is based on the supposition of domesticity as the core of family life" (128).

> The market economy and the advent of capitalism seem to have generated a succession of family changes culminating in the idealization of the nuclear family's domestic seclusion and the division of the sexes into female expressive and male instrumental roles within that family system. Even when the female participates in the labor force, the normative view of her (and very likely her view of herself as well) is a domestic one. (Weitz, 1979: 129)

Early studies on gender roles (for example, Ambert, 1976; Chodorow, 1978; Laws, 1979; Weitz, 1979) established that primary socialization is largely responsible for the eventual imprisonment of adults in roles which limit their achievement in society on the basis of ascribed characteristics, and which colour their attribution of normal or deviant statuses to others. When rigid structural conditions are imposed upon predisposed social actors, such roles become self-perpetuating institutionally as well.

The terms "instrumentality" and "expressivity" reflect not only the nature of prescribed role clusters but also the prescribed settings for their enactment. Instrumental, male activities are played out in the public world of work, finance, and "the market." Expressive, female activities are played out in the private world of home, family, and "domesticity."

More recent feminist writing reveals that such polarization between the public and the private spheres is essential to the maintenance of patriarchy and capitalism (Barrett & McIntosh, 1982; Burstyn & Smith, 1985; Ehrenreich & English, 1978; Luxton & Rosenberg, 1986; Zaretsky, 1976). As Ehrenreich and English put it:

> In the face of the Market, all that is "human" about people must crowd into the sphere of private life, and attach itself, as best it can, to the personal and biological activities which remain there. Only in the home, or private life generally, can one expect to find the love, spontaneity, nurturance or playfulness which are denied in the marketplace. (10)

Luxton and Rosenberg have indicated that women's identities have for generations been offered "through the kitchen window," and women, trapped on the inside, have only recently been working toward establishing identities on the outside. "Woman's place," both in terms of ideological portrayal and cultural practice, continues to be in the domestic sphere. This ideologically-based confluence of role and setting is essential to the understanding of homelessness among women as a social problem.

It is in the "public" sphere of the city that homeless women become visible. The "visibility" or "invisibility" of social types in the public sphere is contingent upon the mediating factor of primary or "master" statuses (Hughes, 1945). For Hughes, individuals may occupy many overlapping, complementary, or competing statuses, but certain statuses, particularly those devalued or deviantized statuses, tend to "rise to the top" and be considered primary. A primary status tends to colour others' interpretations of the individual's entire set of statuses, and "auxilliary" statuses come to support or reinforce the devalued primary status.

In the social construction of the "homeless woman," *gender* is without a doubt the primary status. The individual who is seen to fit the type does so not because she is homeless first, but because she is a *woman* who exhibits certain behaviours that do not mesh with the dominant cultural image of "woman" and "woman's place." As long as women are domestically fixed, are "homeful," they are invisible. Women within the private sphere are isolated and separated, cloaked behind the opaque wall of home. The creation of the homeless woman involves the removal of that wall, the unexpected appearance of women in the public world of the street.

A major factor in this growing visibility is the sheer numbers of women that have been rendered homeless due to the severe housing crisis in major North American cities in the 1980's. Women's housing issues have only recently been addressed in the sociological literature (Bingham, Green & White, 1987; Birch, 1985; Lefkowitz & Withorn, 1986; McClain with Doyle, 1984; Hayden, 1981; Hope & Young, 1986)."Homeless women" have only recently been defined as a social category and hence have only recently become "anomalous" and therefore visible enough to demand domestication (Bahr & Garrett, 1976; Golden, 1979, 1986; Ross, 1982; Rousseau, 1981; Watson with Austerberry, 1986). Homeless men have long held a "place" in the lexicon, a degree of familiarity as part of the urban landscape, and consequently have long been unobtrusive. The "hobo," the "drifter," and the "loner" are positive, romanticized "types" that valorize male freedom in North American culture. Men have, especially in their youth, the institutionalized licence to be visible and mobile, and this is an acceptable route to "self-discovery" (Côté & Levine, 1987). Vagrancy entails a language which typifies *men* as "normal" characters within the setting of skid row. Women, however, have not fit into this typology, and consequently are not perceived as "normally" found in a situation of homelessness. They cannot be dealt with within the language of "skid row," "bum," "rubby," etc. Instead, they require domestication.

As Ross (1982) has pointed out, the anomalous sight of a woman who may appear very poor, alone, and possibly distorted is abhorrent:

> A drunken man is usually ridiculed or ignored, but people are embarrassed and disgusted by the sight of a drunken woman because . . . she negates the symbol of "motherhood," which implies that women are the main stabilizing force in the home and in society. (17)

Despite the apparent strides made by feminism toward challenging patriarchal views on the limits of women's capacities to perform other than "expressive" roles, it is still unusual to see a woman in an uncharacteristic public role or setting. Female bus drivers or police officers are highly visible examples. Typologies of "degraded" female roles in the setting of the street may include "hookers" and "tough broads"; these are ways of seeing public behaviour that have become rigidified, categories that have in many ways come to be accepted, even if the behaviour that they represent does not enjoy widespread moral approval. A woman carrying all of her possessions in a few plastic bags and sleeping in doorways is not immediately acknowledged as being "real," as existing. She cannot be framed within any urban ground rule of roles and settings. We are not accustomed to seeing women "degraded" in this way; the response is to take note and to somehow strive to account for the anomaly.

As recently as 1977, Tindale claimed that women were "not easily found amongst the aged indigent" in a Canadian city (1977:50). The greater visibility of homeless women in recent years can be seen in the increase in the social services for transient women (Cole, 1982; MacLeod, 1980, 1987; Sullivan & Damrosch, 1987; Tierney, 1982), and coverage of the "problem" by sociologists and journalists in the popular press.

Bahr and Garrett "discovered" the disaffiliated urban female in their studies of homelessness in New York in the 1960s. In his foreword to their book, Theodore Caplow provides a thumbnail sketch of this typology, revealing the bias of the functionalist view of the family:

> The disaffiliated woman (living alone, not employed, without voluntary associations) discovered by the research seemed to fall into two general categories: the great majority had been reduced to this wan lifestyle by old age, bereavement, ill health and insufficient income, but for a sizeable minority, disaffiliation culminated a long series of wrong choices and personal failures, drunkenness and desertion, shoplifting and marital violence, abused children and neglected obligations. For this group, strongly represented in the Women's Shelter sample, there is little that anybody can do in the present state of sociological knowledge that would promise more effective rehabilitation than the existing shelter program, which provides bed, board and access to television in a grudging and hostile spirit. The bleakness of the program reflects the hopelessness of the underlying social technology. Something ought to be done about [sic] the bleakness, for decency's sake, but the hopelessness is probably irremovable. (1976:xvi-xvii)

Within this view, homeless women were seen to have brought their troubles upon themselves. This imputation is a form of "blaming the victim" and is an essential ingredient in the functionalist perspective on deviance. A feminist perspective on homelessness, which is offered in this volume, challenges these assumptions and examines the underlying patriarchal hegemony through which homelessness among women is seen as a deficiency which must be corrected.

Homeless women cannot be subsumed indiscriminately under the same rubric that urban ethnographers have used to treat homeless men. There are important differences. The "normal" typology of skid row men held by social scientists holds that they tend to begin the "downward spiral" through alcoholism and failure to maintain respectable ("instrumental") social roles. They tend to be victims of the pressures to maintain respectability within the dominant group, which have driven them to alcoholism. This model applies only to members of the dominant group who had a position to fall from. A sizeable proportion of Canadian street people is made up of Native Canadian Indians, Inuit, and first-generation immigrants (Krotz, 1980; Thrasher, 1976), who experience systematic blocks to mobility which liken them more to homeless women in their lack of conventionally recognized resources. Skid row has long been perceived as a deviant subculture organized around alcoholism and survival, with its own rules of social order, its own identifiable locale ("central business district" and "zone of transition") identified in the early Chicago School studies (Anderson, 1923; Park & Burgess, 1925), and its own institutionalized network of social services (Bahr & Caplow, 1974; Wallace, 1968; Wiseman, 1970).

Homeless women have been "hidden" by their occupation of expressive roles. Most of the transient women who pass through social service centres in a large Ontario city have at one time or another been domestically "fixed": the one organizing factor in their experiences would seem to be a "failure" of the conventional nuclear family arrangement to live up to the mythologized expectations of "home," followed by extreme difficulty in locating and establishing a home of their own. At least half of those seeking shelter at one hostel for women are former mental patients. Others are widows; married women escaping from violent and/or alcoholic husbands; wives left alone as a result of desertion, commitment, or incarceration of their husbands; teenage "runaways"; and single mothers. For these women, "conventional respectability", if they had ever had it, was a status conferred by virtue of their being within a domestic situation in which the responsibility of maintaining respectability was out of their hands. Many married at a time when it was expected that women should not pursue careers outside of the home, but rather that the burden of supporting a home be carried by the husband. Consequently, they raised their families in relative ignorance of what it means to function economically in society, sheltered from the daily exigencies of making money and financing the operation of a family unit. When the economic support falls out of their lives, they are left stranded, helpless, without a home. In most of these cases, women are unprepared to function as economic members of society; ignorant and unskilled at the "instrumental" roles necessary to make their own way back to domesticity. Some enter the condition of homelessness with their children, some alone. Literally "on the street," without a fixed address, without an income, and unable to acquire housing, they join the ranks of the homeless. This was poignantly expressed by one woman who conveyed her experience of rapid loss in status and income when her husband died: "I remember waking up one morning and realizing, 'Oh God, I'm on the skids'."

While data were not available on all of the attributes shared by the women who use shelters, on the basis of my observations and interviews it was apparent that homelessness is experienced by women across social class backgrounds, racial and ethnic backgrounds, and sexual preference. Many of the women encountered were women of colour, primarily of Native Canadian and Caribbean origin.[2] There were quite a few women who were openly lesbian, however they tended to be among the younger clients of the hostel. Several in this category admitted to having run away from home and come to the city in search of an environment where there was more tolerance of their chosen lifestyle.

Of No Fixed Address: Housing as Social Control

Having "no fixed address" is a category used by imputational specialists such as media reporters, police and social workers to domesticate homelessness. The term is used with great frequency in the presentation of "news" (e. g. , "Jane Doe, of no fixed address, was found murdered in a downtown alley," or "John Doe, of no fixed address, is being held for questioning in relation to last night's brutal slaying in a skid row bar"). Such use is testimony to the hegemonic value surrounding one's domestic "rootedness." Having an address *contains* the citizen, makes her accountable. Even "total institutions" (Goffman, 1961) such as prisons and psychiatric care facilities provide a fixed address: they contain social rejects, those who have been defined as having no place in either the public or private spheres. Conventional forms of "civilized," privatized accommodation, such as houses and apartments, *fix* their inhabitants by virtue of their being *numbered*: inhabitants are enumerated as citizens for voting, census, and taxation purposes. The social control implications of being able to locate all members of a group are clear. Correspondingly, the "threat" posed to social control by transient people is akin to that of aliens; homelessness is represented by the media and by social institutions as a form of alienation in our midst.[3]

The tendency of societies to seek to control the homeless is reflected in the history of vagrancy laws (Chambliss, 1964). Since their inception in Britain in 1349, such laws have been used as a way to exercise control over poor and marginal members. Being without visible means of support and without a fixed address are two attributes which are usually allowed as grounds for suspicion: persons exhibiting them are somehow morally unacceptable for not conforming to the dearly held ideals of hard work, property ownership, and family membership. In turn,their "lack" of these attributes implies that they might threaten the interests of the "homeful": vagrants have routinely been arrested as posing a *potential* threat to property (they might steal what they do not have any other means to attain) and family (current Canadian vagrancy laws implicate vagrants as potential child molesters).

Having no fixed address disenfranchises the member. By being deprived of this fundamental right of citizenship, other "rights," particularly those to welfare and employment, are threatened and effectively denied. The homeless find that in order to benefit from welfare and other human services they must meet normative requirements exemplifying a commitment to home, work and family. This results in a kind of hegemonic exclusion which clearly illustrates the power of the language of membership to marginalize those who fail to exhibit their fluency. The language of membership in turn becomes rigidified and translated into rules and laws with the force of official sanction behind them, as in the case of vagrancy laws.

One such rule which reinforces the moral unacceptability of homelessness is that an individual may not receive welfare payments without having a "fixed address" at which to receive her cheque. Finding a fixed address in times of scarce affordable housing is hard enough for anyone on a fixed income, particularly with the trend toward "gentrification" of downtown areas, traditionally the ecological context for low-cost housing. In order to rent a room, first and last months' rent are usually required; in a scarcity situation in which landlords may pick and choose between tenants, many landlords will not rent to individuals who do not have an income. Thus the "Catch-22" of the transient individual: she can not receive welfare money without having a fixed address; she can not afford a fixed address without having amassed considerable "savings" from past welfare payments (a virtual impossibility) or other forms of income. Welfare workers pay close attention to the bank accounts of clients, and may reduce the amount of monthly payments if individuals appear able to "save." This has the net effect of contributing to the widespread problem of homelessness rather than helping to alleviate it.[4]

Visible vs. Invisible Homelessness

Once on the street, homeless women tend to be atomistic. Alcoholism, which drives many skid row men to organize themselves to "go in on a bottle" (Rubington, 1981), is a key to the subculture of homeless men. Homeless women, however, tend to be loners, many of whom are concerned with presenting themselves in a "respectable" manner (maintaining a "neat" appearance, keeping informed by reading the newspaper every day, etc.), evidence of an effort to maintain the *visible* commitment to the dominant normative order by which such things are valued.

There is an institutionalized network of social services providing emergency accommodation for homeless women, in the form of a limited number of hostels offering temporary shelter. After a brief stay, residents are expected to "move on," to "get work," to "find a home." Nevertheless, there is a group of chronic hostel dwellers, called by hostel workers the "regulars," who occupy the "hostel circuit," sometimes for years on end. During this time they are clothed and fed well, and do not appear "visibly homeless." They may subsist as part of the urban landscape, in the public sphere, without "appearing" homeless and thus remain invisible to the deviantizing public gaze.

However, not all homeless women make use of hostels, especially during the warm summer months. This second group, due to living out of doors in poverty, may come to "appear" derelict and thus more visibly homeless. Being "on the street" means that they sleep where they can find shelter: on beaches, in parks, bus stations, public washrooms, doorways. Some turn to prostitution and drug use to provide financial and emotional survival. Each year we hear of some, like the widely publicized case of Drina Jubert, who died of exposure in the cold winter months.[5]

The public perception that the numbers of homeless women are growing is due precisely to their visibility as "out of place." And, as public awareness of the plight of homeless women grows, enhanced primarily through media sensationalism, so does the demand that "something be done"—that they somehow be "given a place" or "put in place." This inevitably translates into a demand for increased social services (Tierney, 1982). Despite close communication between staff at various hostels, and efforts to find beds for all women who come looking for shelter, hostels are frequently forced to turn women away once they have filled their quota. The growth of emergency shelters lags far behind the demand, as evidenced by the chronic shortage of beds.

The societal response to the situation of homeless women must be critically examined. While there is no denying that shelters are serving an important service, it is simply myopic to accept that they are either designed for, or capable of, any ultimate solution of the problem. There is a risk that social services will continue to rise to meet the perceived "increase" in numbers of transient women in the same way that they have accommodated transient men, getting larger and larger, simply providing a place to "flop" and nothing more. An even more serious implication is that the category "homeless woman" may be uncritically subsumed into the common-sense lexicon and under the rubric of the sociology of deviance.

We must become aware of how homeless women construct their own social reality and in turn how imputational specialists construct the social reality of homelessness and attempt to reconstruct "homefulness," for these two conceptions are very closely linked. What is it about the conventional home that has caused these women to become "homeless"? What does it mean, in turn, to "have a home"? The attribution of deficiency, through which it is assumed that homeless women have failed their families, is precisely rooted in a conception of domesticity which is stubbornly inflexible. Perhaps it is the "nuclear family," as an obsolescent institution that is under considerable stress as increasingly unrealistic demands are placed upon it to conform with the myth of home, that is failing. If the conventional home as a desirable form of social organization is on the wane, then perhaps it is time that we ceased regarding the homeless as "failures" and began to regard the whole notion of home as problematic.

The Myth of Home

The creation of the "homeless woman" is indicative of key elements of the normative structure. Of these I will look to two: the "mythologization" of home; and the vested interest in creating "homelessness" in order to oppositionally create "homefulness."

The increasing visibility of homeless women has as much to do with increasing numbers as with the creation and use of the category itself. This has been incorporated into the public/media/professional lexicon in part to account for what is perceived as a "new" social problem. More importantly, it is through incorporation of this term that the social problem has been "domesticated." Homelessness is a real threat to the cultural iconography of a changing society for which "home" itself is becoming increasingly ambiguous.

"Home" in our culture means a fixed place of residence shared with others, characterized by warmth, safety, security, and emotional dependence, implying privacy and intimacy. In Western capitalist, patriarchal society it has long been associated with private property and intimate nuclear familial relations (Zaretsky, 1976). Such an ideal sets up "home" as a distinctly desirable, domestic, sedentary situation of familiarity. With the hegemonic aid of the mass media, educational, political, judicial, and religious institutions, the monolithic middle-class monogamous, stable nuclear family has remained a cultural ideal.

Home is embodied in our language by an inviolable myth: that of "domestic bliss." Anything that might violate that ideal, that might in some way serve to "break up the family"—from child abuse to infidelity to wife battering to desertion, whether originating from within or without—is met with great resistance by social service agencies, the mass media, and public opinion. Yet the myth strains against the inevitability of social change. There has been a general move away from rigidly defined "expressive" roles for women; however, a consequence of this has been a large degree of role ambiguity for both women and men. Women flooding the work force have encountered difficulties, not only in redefining themselves vis-à-vis the expressive selves that they were socialized to be, but also in redefining themselves vis-à-vis the instrumental roles, occupied by men, that they have been led recently to desire (Armstrong, 1984).

Change in the form as well as the content of home has been occurring at an ever increasing rate. The form of home as being a fixed residence of private property may remain an ideal, but one that is increasingly remote. With geographical mobility necessitated by the interchangeability of employees has come the interchangeability of domiciles (Packard, 1972). In times of astronomical rises in property value, home ownership has been challenged by the greater convenience and economy of tenancy. The warmth and emotional stability mythologized as characterizing the home may also remain an ideal, yet for many it is unrealizeable in a context of escalating rates of divorce and domestic violence.

The stable, nuclear-family-based notion of home has become less and less the norm.[6] Alternative forms of living arrangements appear in which commitment is redefined from fixed to transient spatial and family relations. As Eichler (1983) argues, these alternatives are resulting in the "household" rather than the "home" being the basis for rootedness. The development of accepted "singles" lifestyles is one outcome of this phenomenon.[7] Alternatives to the traditional familiar primary group now include commuter marriages, childless or late childbearing marriages, common-law marriages, single-parent homes, gay and lesbian households, and co-operative sharing of living space among unrelated others; but even these are viewed by imputational specialists as temporary, deviant, or at the very least morally inferior to the idealized nuclear family.

These empirical changes in living arrangements do not conform with the "traditional" idealization of home, which is firmly rooted in an obsolescent gendered division of labour within the nuclear family. "Domestic bliss" as an image to which members aspire can only lead to sadness, disappointment, and a sense of moral deficiency when it is not achieved. Within such an inflexible "role set," a woman who does not occupy the mythologized position of wife and mother lacks a place, posing a threat to that very myth. It follows that it is the very enormity of change away from the rigidly defined version of "home" that has produced the visibly "homeless" woman, along with the imperative of giving her a name, and therefore of giving her a place. It is perhaps not coincidental that social policy makers and implementers have adopted "domestication" as the mode of dealing with any challenge to that myth. Language is the only way that a homeless society can relate to an anomalous situation, because to "domesticate" it—to appropriate, bring home, and control—is to fit it into a reality for which familiarity, in the form of the urban ground rule of the language of membership, has come to *replace the familiarity of home.*

So not only does "domestication" become the most fitting relation to a social problem, but it also becomes clear how the "homeless woman" may be created. Not only has observation replaced participation; reading replaced speaking; transiency replaced permanency; but the language of membership exists to preserve the image of another world, long gone. The domestication of the homeless woman is the bringing home and controlling of an image which represents a deep fear—a fear of the end of the family, the end of privacy, ultimately the end of patriarchy. The homeless woman is a symbol of everything that is closing in upon the urban dweller, of every fear that is aroused by the elusiveness of home. To pinpoint her as "homeless" is to define ourselves as "homeful"; to domesticate homelessness is to make it accountable, identifiable as a "normal" social problem that *others* have, others who have clearly *failed* at domesticity. So we in turn domesticate her and provide a new place, a new version of home in the guise of help. It is to the process of reproducing domesticity through the provision of human services for homeless women that we must now turn.

Notes

1. This chapter is a significantly reworked version of Lesley D. Harman (1987b), "The creation of the 'Bag lady': Rethinking home for homeless women," Human Affairs 12:58-86.

2. Women of Oriental origin were notably absent from the sample. It would be interesting to explore the relationship between the cultural strength of the family unit among various immigrant groups, and the degree of homelessness among women, particularly the elderly.

3. In preparation for the 1988 elections in both Canada and the United States, some efforts were made to allow for the enumeration of the homeless. As individual franchise is so closely tied to home ownership, however, the obstacles to be overcome are enormous indeed.

4. At the time of the study, it was often the case that emergency welfare funds could be secured to aid women in getting a place of their own. According to hostel staff, this practise has been discontinued in the case of women, due to the perception that while they are in the care of hostels they have all of their basic needs supplied and do not need any extra money. this type of regressive practice is disturbing in that it demonstrated state efforts to domesticate homelessness and effectively reduce opportunities for women to extricate themselves from the downward spiral of chronic homelessness.

5. Drina Jubert was discovered dead in an abandoned truck in Toronto in December of 1985, having frozen to death at the age of 41. Media accounts of her death focused on the fact that as a young woman "her picture appeared in advertisements and she was offered the chance of a film career" (Taylor, 1986, p. A1). That she had gone from that "type of life", which celebrated female beauty and sexuality, to the alcoholic life of a "bag lady," "moving from hostel to hostel, or living on the street," was depicted as the ultimate in her failure as a woman.

6. Recent estimates suggest that only 10 to 15 per cent of Canadian citizens live in this type of household (Eichler, 1983).

7. The AIDS epidemic is currently serving as a powerful deterrent to spontaneous sex with multiple partners, pointing to the revival of monogamy or celibacy as desired living arrangements.

Chapter Two

Patriarchy and Social Policy: Hostels for Homeless Women

If social problems are constructed through challenges to the normative structure, then the demand that "something be done" must follow too. Formal social control of deviants is the legitimate concern of the state in capitalist society. The creation and implementation of social policy, then, can be seen to mirror state ideology. Public policy over "private" domains constitutes an intrusion of the state into "private" lives and a translation of those lives into the domain of the "social" (Donzelot, 1979). Social control over the family, and over relations of production and reproduction, accounts for a large proportion of state activities. This chapter investigates the implications of the relationship between the dominant ideology of patriarchy and the implementation of social policy in the provision of services for homeless women. It will be argued that these services tend to mirror and reinforce patriarchal assumptions about "woman's place" in relation to the home.

Patriarchy, the State, and Social Policy
A remarkable thing about capitalist society is its hegemonic commitment to the autonomy of both household and economy. In this intersection of realms, there are two social institutions which Dickinson and Russell (1986) point to as pivotal: household and state, corresponding to private and public life.

Zaretsky's influential book, *Capitalism, the Family, and Personal Life* (1976), identifies the development of capitalism as the source of the distinction between private and public realms, noting that previously family and economy were one.

> This "split" between the socialized labour of the capitalist enterprise and the private labour of women in the home is closely related to a second "split"—between our "personal" lives and our place within the social division of labour. (29)

In their study of changing definitions of "woman's place," Ehrenreich and English (1978) focus on shifting relations between the public and private, and explain that "the two spheres stand, in respect to their basic values, *opposed* to each other, and the line between them is charged with moral tension" (9). The opposition between public and private is located precisely in the demands placed upon women and men to occupy certain roles in the fulfillment of the demands of the different spheres. As suggested in Chapter One, it is in the ideologically-produced confluence of role and setting that we can understand the power of the image of "woman's place" in the myth of home.

The myth of home has been predicated on the notion that the public world is a cold, savage place where men engage in the aggressive, competitive and instrumental struggle for economic survival. Against that world stands the spectre of home, the domain of woman. Domesticity becomes synonymous with warmth, nurturance, and expressivity, and the historical development of the two distinct spheres comes to be seen as "natural."

> Rather than working for a corporation the housewife worked for a particular man, for herself, and for their children and relatives. Housework and child-rearing came to be seen as natural or personal functions performed in some private space outside society.
>
> (Zaretsky, 1976: 81)

Public and private spheres are linked through economic and social ties of production, consumption, and biological and social reproduction. Workers in the public sphere engage in production of commodities, and their wages are geared for the provision of the means for consumption of these goods, as well as the necessities of survival. The household is the context for both biological and social reproduction. Biologically, the species is reproduced through childbearing. Socially, class and gender divisions are reproduced through childrearing. Control over both biological and social reproduction is clearly in the interests of the dominant group (patriarchal monopoly capital), and it is precisely at their intersection, and with the shifting distinctions between public and private realms, that intervention in the form of state social policy, flourishes.

An essential element in the enduring patterns of patriarchal relations is that of women's dependency on men. This dependency mirrors the public/private split in role domains. Men's control of the public domain provides them with legitimacy as earners ("breadwinners"), and by implication women's exclusion from the public domain results in any claim to economic independence being viewed as illegitimate. Conscripted to the "private" domain, women are in turn dependent upon men's earning power in the public domain in order to carry out their duties as homemakers and caregivers. As Smith (1985) notes:

No matter how it is done, where men are wage earners and women cannot earn enough outside the home to provide for their children independently of a man and his wage, dependency permeates every aspect of the interpersonal process in the home. (6)

She asserts that "dependency is part of a perpetuated pattern of excluding women and married women in particular from functioning as independent economic agents" (27).

A cornerstone of patriarchal social structure is that, as traditionally conceptualized, the family is the "backbone of civilization" (O'Brien, 1981). The future of society can only be guaranteed through the maintenance of a stable, nurturing private realm in which personal and emotional growth can be assured. The world without home, in other words, is a world without love. In social policy this is translated into the prioritizing of measures which will preserve, replace, or reproduce such environmental conditions where they are viewed by imputational specialists to be somehow "deficient."

With greater state intervention in the regulation of family life, there has been a movement from "family patriarchy" to "state patriarchy" (Ursel, 1986). Ursel makes distinctions between three different types of patriarchy, depending on the dominant economic and gender power relations of the time: communal patriarchy (with men-as-a-class having control over women-as-a-class in pre-class, kin-based society); family patriarchy (with individual males having control over individual women in class-based, preindustrial society); and social patriarchy (with the state having control over the reproductive units in advanced wage labour systems). These distinctions can be identified through different modes of social policy aimed at reproducing prevailing gender norms. And in the transition between the different orders can be seen the mobilization of patriarchal forces to ensure "woman's place" in the "balancing of the productive/reproductive needs of society" (164).

The provision of human services must be examined in light of both their "manifest" and "latent" functions (Merton, 1968). In reviewing a particular social service response to a perceived social problem, one must consider the explicitly stated goals of the program, as well as the way in which the program is administered, and finally the perhaps unintended consequences for the lives and experiences of the recipients of the services.

The provision of human services in Canada by federal, provincial, and municipal governments is informed by the principle that every citizen is entitled to certain fundamental ingredients to subsistence living, and that, when individuals are unable to provide for themselves, the state assumes the role of *parens patriae*: a parental figure taking responsibility for the welfare of its dependents. While the term *parens patriae* is typically associated with the guardianship role of the state in caring for young offenders and children in need of protection, it is also appropriate in the understanding of the sense of duty and obligation underlying the contemporary welfare state (Black, 1979: 1003). This understanding may be furthered by recognizing another important principle, that of *patria potestas*, which refers to paternal authority of a man over his wife and children. *Patria potestas* has provided the norm for relations both within and without the family in patriarchal, capitalist society. It is predicated on the common-law understanding that women and children are the chattels of men, and can be dealt with within the private sphere with relative impunity from the state. It is only recently, with steadily increasing family legislation, that the state has come to penetrate the opaque wall of the private sphere to regulate domestic relations (Harman, 1988).

The state can be seen to be assuming a role of *patria potestas* within *parens patriae*. Not only does the state become "like the parent" to citizens in need of aid, but within the tradition of patriarchy it also becomes "like the father." With this combination, it can be seen that the "myth of home" is reproduced within services for homeless women.

The kinds of fundamental human needs that are generally regarded as essential are covered by the three categories of human services identified by Wineman (1984): economic assistance, psychosocial services, and residential care. Economic assistance entails the provision of "basic material needs either through direct income assistance or through subsidies of various sorts" (37); it includes such services as welfare, disability insurance, unemployment insurance, health insurance, public housing, and pensions. Psychosocial services are those "in which professionals attempt to help 'clients' to overcome problems in living...[and] span a continuum from purely voluntary to explicitly coerced participation by 'clients'" (43); they include such services as psychological counselling, behaviour modification, and drug and alcohol treatment. Residential care settings "are total living situations in which a set of paid caretakers assumes control over and responsibility for the residents' lives" (47); they include institutions such as foster homes, training schools, psychiatric care facilities, halfway houses, and homes for the aged and the chronically ill.

If we can begin to see relations between patriarchy, the family, and the state as being far from accidental, then we can begin to see that the formal imputation and treatment of "deviance" among women is structurally produced as well. This is nowhere more striking than in social service responses to homelessness among women.

In their study of homeless women in London, England, Watson and Austerberry (1986) grapple with the difficulty of defining "homelessness" as it is experienced by women. They make a useful distinction between "concealed" homelessness, which is found among single women who stay with friends or make other temporary living arrangements, and "institutionalized" homelessness, through which social services such as hostels and emergency shelters are utilized. Their third category, "potential" homelessness, may become manifested in either the former or the latter if conditions exist which provide women with either the opportunity or the necessity of becoming homeless.

"Concealed" homelessness, taking place as it does within the context of someone else's home or some other "legitimate" living arrangement (such as working as a live-in domestic, for example), belongs to the private realm. "Institutionalized" homelessness is more "visible" and tends to be the target of social policy. For the purpose of this study, the condition of homelessness is seen to be exemplified by the very presence of women in social services for homeless women. Having defined themselves as in need of shelter and social assistance, they are *ipso facto* defined as homeless by those supplying those services.

Those making up the complement of "homeless women" share the attribution of failure at expressive roles: supportive wife, nurturing mother, competent and undemanding homemaker. "Homelessness" in essence refers to having lost—or perhaps never having had—one's place in the "private" realm. Whether one "broke away" willingly or was cast out by forces beyond one's control, the appearance of the homeless woman in the public world implies a kind of poverty of gender—one has failed as a woman. The adjective "homeless" itself, as an "achieved" attribute, describes achievement through loss: one's lack of a key ingredient to gender identity provides one with a primary status which becomes the equivalent of "failure." If women have failed at being dependent-expressive, then what could they possibly be good for?

Over half of the women appearing at the hostel in this study had been institutionalized at one point for "mental illness." The literature on women and mental illness (for example, Chesler, 1972; Sampson, Messinger & Towne, 1962; Schur, 1984; Szasz, 1974) indicates that the labeling of women as mentally ill is routinely associated with their perceived failure in expressive roles. The processing of women as mental patients effectively relinquishes their expressive *superior* passive-dependent roles within the family, replacing them with expressive *inferior* passive-dependent roles as mental patients. The massive over prescription of tranquilizers and other drugs to noninstitutionalized women in North America serves as an intermediary between the home and the hospital. In the guise of "help," extensive drug use serves the interests of the state in maintaining women's compliance within the home.

The release from mental institutions often results in temporary, if not "permanent," transiency on behalf of female out-patients and ex-patients. Transitional housing is not always available for them, and many have difficulty in functioning on their own after having been institutionalized, and hence made dependent, for an extended period of time. Many such informants admitted to "feeling better now," but at the expense of having "all the life taken out of me" through a constant state of being drugged. Passed from institution to institution, dependency to dependency, they find themselves inured to the passage of time, to the world around them, unmotivated to make any change. "Why bother?" is the resounding answer to the impertinent question, "Why don't you do something about your life?"

The recent emphasis on bringing wife battering "out of the closet" in an effort to halt the societal practise of blaming the victim—shared by common-sense members, media, police, lawyers, and judges alike—attests to the deep entrenchment of the equation between *battered* and *failure*. As many authors (for example, Cole, 1982; MacLeod, 1980, 1987; Martin, 1977; Tierney, 1982) have noted, there is a tendency for women to feel shame and guilt when battered, interpreting the beating as punishment for having "failed". Women who have left destructive relationships—violent, alcoholic, or emotionally abusive—are reaching for a way out of their oppressive situations, yet through the institutionalized practice of "victim blaming" are led to feel morally deficient, often returning to the relationship after having had little success in finding housing and financial and social support.

Tierney (1982) traces the development of the "battered women movement" and notes that it was only after considerable agitation by women's groups in the early 1970s that "wife battering" became recognized as a social problem by media, public, and government, and that social services were mobilized to provide shelters for victims of such battering. The phenomenal growth of such services—from none to over three hundred shelters in the U. S. within six years—indicates the undeniability of the need to respond to what had suddenly become a national issue.

This unprecedented growth of shelters for battered women would seem to speak to the relation between the promise of feminism and the mobilization of social service resources to come to the aid of women in need. But what kind of care do they provide? Wineman's (1984) categories of types of human services, while useful in conceptualizing the different forms that the provision of human services may take, prove somewhat rigid when applied to the emergency hostel. Hostels can be viewed as providing economic assistance, in that the basic needs of shelter, food, clothing, and transportation are provided free of charge to the residents. They may also be classed as offering psychosocial services, as the staff members often have social work training and are available to consult with residents about their problems. Finally, they may be seen as residential care settings because for the time of residential stay, they constitute total institutions (Goffman, 1961) in which the dependency of homeless women becomes clearly visible and reinforced.

One reason for the ambiguity regarding what type of service the hostel constitutes is that hostels vary in their philosophies toward giving care. Another is the large gap that may be perceived between its manifest and latent functions. Manifestly, the hostel is intended to replace a home on a temporary basis. In this sense, it should provide all of the "comforts of home" including the necessities for survival, emotional warmth, and a helping, healing environment for women in need. According to the stated goals of the hostel, it would constitute a blend of economic and psychosocial assistance. However, as we shall see,the latent function of hostels is to reproduce domesticity in a context of dependency and control, and thus we find very little effective psychosocial assistance, despite the best intentions of hostel staff. Rather, the latent effect of the hostel is to combine economic assistance and long-term residential care for the chronically homeless. This has the effect of reproducing patriarchal relations.

Research on women and social policy (Lefkowitz & Withorn, 1986; Olson, 1985; Sapiro, 1985; Ungerson, 1985; Ursel, 1986; Watson with Austerberry, 1986; Wilson, 1977) testifies to the prevalence of the patriarchal bias in the treatment of women. The recently outlawed "man in the house" rule—making a single mother ineligible for mother's allowance benefits if she appears to be sexually involved with a man who might sleep at her home—is a case in point. The underlying patriarchal assumption is that if there is a man in the house then he (as the "breadwinner") should support the woman (Fairbairns, 1985). This implies that state support is offered *in place of* the support of a man: state-provided public support in lieu of male-provided public support. *Parens patriae* is also evident when, as is often the case, single mothers are expected to stay home with their children and not encouraged to work and become self-sufficient. In the case of homeless women, we may find a similar pattern.

The very model of a "shelter" implies that the shelter takes on an instrumental role and the woman retains an expressive role: dependency has been displaced from the family to the source of shelter. Further analysis reveals, however, that there is also a *downward spiral* entailed in this displacement, through which the woman may undergo *status* displacement as well.

In the following chapters, it will be argued that the hostel has the effect of reproducing domesticity for homeless women. This domesticity provides the warmth and security of home on a temporary basis for those who will be fortunate enough to have a "fresh start" to their lives, but it also becomes a context for domesticating a segment of homeless women who become known as "regulars." For these chronically homeless women, the system encourages a destructive kind of dependency that makes it increasingly difficult for them to pull themselves out of the downward spiral of homelessness.

Chapter Three

Becoming a Volunteer:
An Ethnographic Approach to Studying
Homeless Women

The prospect of studying various dimensions of the experiences of homeless women poses methodological difficulties and concerns for the sociologist. Having made the decision to explore the world of homeless women, I was faced with many questions as to how to proceed. How would I "operationalize" the concept of "homeless women"? How would I find them? How would I present myself? What form of sampling, data collection, and analysis would be most appropriate for this particular population? My preference was for a qualitative approach. I sought to understand their world using the techniques of ethnography and grounded theory (Glaser & Strauss, 1967).

Choosing a Method
The question of what method to use in studying homeless women was answered by the population itself. The first problem that presented itself was, how to identify the population? Homeless people do not have any of the standard attributes used to identify target samples. They can not be reached through random mailings or through random selection of telephone numbers. They do not appear in census data, they do not all receive welfare cheques, they do not pay taxes. They do not own cars, have drivers' licenses, credit cards, or often even bank accounts. Homeless women are, by and large, outside of the mainstream economy and the system of social control by which citizens' activities are monitored. Some may view this as a kind of ultimate freedom from the surveillance of the state, a kind of social invisibility by which people may actually, for all intents and purposes, "not exist. "

Yet we know that the homeless exist because they are not afforded the kind of invisibility that private property, particularly in the form of home ownership, provides. The homeless are visible on the urban landscape precisely because they lack shelter in the conventional sense in which citizens are taught to think of it. They appear anomalous sleeping in public. They obtrude into public places and paradoxically offend the propriety of citizens who view public property as predicated on the understanding that those who use it are just "passing through" on the way to or from home, who believe that public and private realms can be neatly and conveniently separated.

When contemplating this study, I conferred with some colleagues who suggested that I "pass" as a bag lady on the street and learn the culture that way. This approach appealed to them as being genuine, covert participant observation that would be sure to give me a true glimpse into the underworld of the homeless. I did not choose this option for a number of important reasons. I considered it highly unethical to go "under cover" in this case. If the world of homelessness did indeed provide a kind of anonymity, a kind of freedom from surveillance, then the last thing I was prepared to do was to intrude on that world, uninvited. How would I know a homeless woman when I saw her? Operationalizing the concept of "homeless" is difficult, and my selection of subjects would have been coloured by media-produced conceptions of what a "bag lady" looked like (for example, Cuff, 1981). This could also pose problems of personal health and safety, which I was unwilling to risk. Illness and disease, particularly in the form of tuberculosis, plague the homeless, and the lifestyle also does little to discourage infestations by fleas and lice of bedding, clothing, and hair. Violence is not unheard of, and I felt it would be foolhardy to venture naively onto the turf of street people.

It became evident that in order to satisfy these concerns, I would have to seek out a safe, controlled setting in which individuals had defined themselves as homeless. The first environment that came to mind was the emergency hostel. The emergency shelter exists to provide a temporary haven for women. In order to be admitted, the woman generally has to take the first step by defining herself as in need of help, and admitting herself to the hostel. This would provide a very specific, self-selected sample: women who defined themselves as wanting and needing shelter. The subjects would, in other words, define themselves. While clearly this would not tap all "homeless" women, it would provide a context from which to begin to understand the experiences of women within the hostel system.

There were many women who could be termed "homeless" who would not be included in this sample. First, women living on the street who did not seek out social service assistance, who may in fact have defined themselves as homeless but were uninterested in or unaware of hostels, would not be included. Second, the "concealed homeless"— sheltered women who may not have had a conventional "home" and may have considered themselves "homeless," but who may not have come to the attention of social service agencies—would not be included.

Third, the "potentially homeless"—women who sought to leave unde-sirable home lives but had "nowhere to go"—would not be included (Watson with Austerberry, 1986: 21).

While the first of these three categories would be untapped for reasons outlined above, the second and third categories are invisible for reasons that are central to a feminist understanding of homelessness. The "con-cealed homeless" are likely to be in their situation due to a cumulation of factors similar to those which produce homelessness among other women. They may be institutionalized in psychiatric care facilities or prisons. When released from such facilities, many women find them-selves on the street without the familial or financial support to rees-tablish conventional homes. Or they may be staying with family or friends as a default option due to the unavailability of affordable hous-ing. This is usually interpreted as failure, for within our culture it generally means failure as a "wife" and "mother. " The "potentially homeless" may in fact be trapped within "conventional homes" as a default option for the same reasons. In both categories, these women are generally on the edge of homelessness, straddling the tight rope between acceptability and oblivion. Yet they are well hidden and often see the hostel as a last resort. They would be left out of my sample, part of the "dark figure of homelessness" that I would leave to others to explore.

Having identified the context for my study, and the sample, the next problem would be how to collect the data. Because of the inevitably small sample, any type of survey research was out of the question. I hoped to be as unobtrusive as possible, slipping in and absorbing as much knowledge as I could. This could only be accomplished through a combination of participant observation and in-depth interviews.

The principle behind participant observation is that one enters a foreign culture as a stranger, and learns the meanings and motives of members of that culture from the inside. By observing and partaking in the everyday, routine activities of the culture, the observer develops an understanding based on experience which is grounded in the culture itself (Harman, 1987a; Spradley, 1980). In-depth interviews with subjects allow the researcher to pursue her understanding by seeking clarifica-tion of the language, as well as developing close personal ties with members which often serve to facilitate the integration of the researcher into the community. Ethical issues must always be on the researcher's mind, and every effort made to avoid harm to either subjects or re-searcher.

Recent contributions by feminists to the literature on fieldwork show the growing influence of feminist methodologies on the ways in which sociologists may utilize the fieldwork experience as a context for praxis (Warren, 1988). From a feminist perspective, the ideal of the detached, rational, objective observer is a patriarchal myth. Instead, the feminist approach to fieldwork advocates involvement in the emotional and political lives of the people under study.

> There has been a general movement in both sociology and anthropology, animated by a socialist, humanist, or religious concern for the plight of the world's oppressed people, to engage in research only if there is the probability of some outcome beneficial to the people studied. Feminists whose politics are linked to these movements but focused on women are interested in linking their research activities to succor for women in our own and other cultures. (Warren, 1988: 40)

Having been initially trained in the classical, male-stream school of participant observation, I had misgivings about how appropriate that methodology would be in terms of handling the real life dramas that I would inevitably encounter in my contact with homeless women. I resolved to keep myself open at all times to my subjects; to get close to them, to help them when I could, and ultimately to learn as much as possible about their situation from the inside.

The choice of participant observation, and the keen awareness of the ethical questions involved, made the decision of what role to take a crucial one. If I posed as a homeless woman *within* such a setting, would this be ethical? Again, "passing" was suggested to me and again I decided, no. I had several hunches about the "inside" world of hostels, but had never set foot in one before. I suspected that there might be some kind of "community," perhaps even a subculture, predicated on a certain code for membership involving trust and mutual acceptance. For reasons similar to those militating against passing as a street person, I elected not to intrude. If I was not going to pass as a homeless woman, perhaps I should attempt to pass as a social worker and gather my data in that way. But aside from significant misrepresentation (I had a Ph. D. in sociology, not training in the delivery of social services) and red tape involved in taking on such a role, I felt that this role would polarize my relationships with the women and not give me an opportunity to pursue the in-depth interviews that I sought. I could not imagine stepping into this world and pretending to a certain cultural competence that I had yet to learn. It would be extremely difficult to carry out the dual roles of authority figure and empathic observer without a degree of conflict, and possible failure at both. I presumed that the women would be accustomed to being treated as subjects, as social services generally require that "face sheet data" be gathered on those making use of facilities. I also presumed that there would be a power differential between those collecting the data and those providing them, which might bias the information that I would receive.

In the end, I opted for a marginal, unobtrusive role as a volunteer worker. This seemed optimal, in that it would allow me to be "green" as I learned the role, without jeopardizing the health or safety of subjects;

it would allow me to learn the structure and relationships of the hostel from the inside; it would allow me to get to know subjects in a caring, empathic way without the added constraints of an authority role; it would allow me to have contact with both clients and staff; and finally, it would allow me considerable flexibility to come and go as I pleased.

Choosing a Hostel

When I began the study, there were thirteen emergency hostels for women in the target city. They were not all the same. Some were specifically for battered women; some took families, including men; some were directed toward teenagers. Some were state-run, some private; some were based on the strict Christian "mission" spirit, some were more tolerant and even openly feminist in their attempts to help women. I sought a shelter that had a very open policy, such that any woman defining herself as in need of shelter could be admitted. The shelter chosen was predicated on a strong feminist philosophy of self-help and empowerment, run for and by women, with the staff displaying a deep commitment to helping women help themselves. In many ways the staff consider this shelter to be an alternative to the patriarchal models followed by most others, and it is, therefore, not to be seen as representative of all.[1]

I approached the hostel staff and was informed that they received daily requests, primarily from social work students, to study their clients. The staff, evidencing a deep concern for the protection of their clients, were quite reluctant to allow any outsiders in because, as I was told, "People live here; this is their home." I was invited to a staff meeting to plead my case, and discovered that my chosen method appealed to the staff members. They cautioned me not to appear "with a clip board" and try to administer questionnaires to the women. I was told of an experience in which a prominent social worker had done just that. The staff reported that the residents had found the experience to be alienating, had not co-operated, and that the attempt had failed miserably. When I assured them that my approach would be noninterventionist, they relaxed and allowed that I be put through the volunteer training program and given an opportunity to conduct the study. The staff reserved the right to terminate my access to the hostel at any time.

The major hurdle, as it turned out, was not in gaining entrance to the hostel but in gaining clearance from the ethics committee of the university at which I held my fellowship. While the committee members reluctantly agreed that participant observation could be used, they insisted on "informed consent" for any interviews. "Informed consent," as it is typically understood for the purposes of conducting sociological and psychological research, involves the subjects signing a form in which they are made aware of the intentions of the study, of the confidentiality of the data, and of their right to cease involvement at any time. While I had no problem with guaranteeing that the subjects had this information, it was entirely inconsistent with the type of sample and the methodology employed to use consent forms. My aim was precisely to get around the "clip board" image that seemed to hold such a negative association. I was also concerned that, in light of the anonymity that homelessness provides, many women would be unwilling to sign a form, and in fact the study could be severely jeopardized by this requirement. If my aim was to develop trusting relationships, it was very possible that the standard consent forms could diminish rather than augment this trust.

I proposed a compromise to the committee: when conducting taped in-depth interviews I would begin by asking the subject if she minded if the interview were taped, tell her that I was seeking to explore the world of homelessness and hostels, that all information conveyed would be confidential, but that I may wish to provide anonymous quotations when the findings were published. Finally, I would tell her that she should feel free to answer only questions with which she was comfortable and the interview could end at any time she desired. The committee accepted this.

Becoming a Volunteer

"Getting in" to a research setting involves more than passing the gate-keepers (in this case, hostel staff and ethics committee). It involves finding a role and establishing oneself and one's credibility. As many accounts show (Shaffir, Stebbins, & Turowetz, 1980), this is often the most difficult stage, and also the most important. It is difficult in that it entails the total immersion of the observer in an alien environment, a different culture. It is essential that the observer quickly "learn the ropes" in order not to appear obtrusive. It is important because mistakes made at this stage can do irreparable damage to the researcher's chances of gaining the trust of her subjects.

For me, "getting in" entailed two quite different but inseparable steps. First, I needed to learn how the hostel operated so that I could function as a volunteer and thus assume my role. Second, I needed to learn to feel comfortable in the hostel environment. As it turned out, the second task proved far more difficult than the first.

I was given a day-long introduction to the structure of the hostel. This entailed an initial interview wherein I was informed of the feminist philosophy behind the hostel, the role of the volunteers, staff, and clients. I was shown the intake sheets and witnessed an intake interview. I was taken through the house, room by room—shown fire exits, extinguishers, alarms. I was given a set of keys which allowed entry into privileged places: the food storage room, the laundry room, the donations room, the basement meeting room, the staff office. I was made to feel familiar with the house; with imaginary map in hand, the next step was to feel comfortable socially.

Every researcher who engages in participant observation knows how important it is to be able to have a place to go to get away from the "front region" (Goffman, 1959) of the field setting. For me, this place was the staff room. It quickly became like a sanctuary to me. It was a highly controlled territory which residents generally entered only with permission, usually when they wanted something (drugs, tokens, sundries, tobacco) over which the staff had supervision, or when they needed help or advice. It was a kind of neutral zone in which I was out of view of my subjects, a kind of "back region. " Whenever things got overwhelming, whenever I wanted to escape to record observations, whenever I wanted to ask questions about proper procedure or bounce ideas around, I retreated to the warm, considerate acceptance of the staff room. But there I was marginal as well. As a matter of necessity, the staff themselves had developed a close-knit subculture. While always helpful and patient with me, I nevertheless always knew that I was not one of them.

Against the safe, predictable atmosphere of the staff room was the other side of the door, with all of the unpredictable elements that go along with a new culture. The first day in the hostel, I did not know what to expect when I went into the kitchen and offered to help. With my upper middle-class background and attendant sense of propriety, I felt trepidation, almost fear at encountering the unknown. Walking into the kitchen, I found two residents hunched over at the table, silently smoking, drinking coffee, holding their heads in their hands. This was my first exposure to the practice of "passing time" that is so prevalent among those who make use of hostels. It made me immediately aware that there was going to be much more to this "getting in" process than met the eye. I would have to rethink the very assumptions I had about "what one does with one's time. " For an aggressive, compulsive academic who generally viewed days and weeks as far too short to accommodate all I had to do, this was to be a difficult task.

Another assumption I had to rethink was that of the "conversational mutuality" that pervades the highly verbal world of academe. I began to realize how much of my time I spent talking: to students and colleagues during the work day; to my spouse, family and friends at other times. Having so much to talk about is an indication in itself of the degree of involvement that one has with various role clusters and responsibilities. The simple distinction between "home" and "work" and the attendant use of the opposite setting as a basis for sharing conversation (e. g. "What did you do at work today?" being asked when one comes "home," or "How are things at home?" being asked when one chats with a colleague at work, etc.) is taken for granted by those who have access to both realms and by implication do "interesting things" during the day.

Trying to make conversation with the women in the kitchen that day proved to be excruciatingly difficult. They simply were not interested. I awkwardly asked questions like, "What is your name?" "How do you like the hostel?" "What do you think of the food they serve here?" and received one-word answers. The women remained slouched over, did not make eye contact with me, and my initial, tenuous cheeriness gave way to growing concern about how I was going to learn what to talk about. As I came to be known as someone who could be trusted and talked to, this changed. But I found, again and again, that the women often turned the conversation to *me*, so that they could hear about *my* life, which, as boring and monotonous as I felt my life as a scholar usually was, they saw to be exciting and challenging.

The initial shock of facing the world of the homeless told me much about what I took for granted as normal modes of interaction, and also directed my attention to questions like, "What do the women do with their time?" and "What do they talk about?" as I slowly got into their world and began asking questions and conducting in-depth interviews.

The first day I only lasted two very long hours. I went home and slept for twelve hours and woke up severely depressed, weeping uncontrollably. I had found myself overwhelmed by the enormous gap I perceived between my world and the world of the homeless women; I wondered if I could ever overcome it, and felt defeated from the beginning. Despite having presented myself in a way that conformed to the dress of the staff (jeans, sweatshirt, running shoes), I stood out awkwardly. A woman coming into the kitchen had remarked, "You're new, aren't you? Well, you'll get the hang of it"; she had picked up on my politeness, my obvious lack of familiarity with the subculture, and my close adherence to the formal house rules.

Yet I had also felt a strange comfort in that kitchen, one that was to grow as the months went by. As the staff room was one kind of sanctuary, the kitchen became another. The kitchen was the centre of much activity in the house: a meeting place, a place in which power relations were established, in which weekly battles were fought. It was the residents' territory, like the staff room was the staff's territory. And I learned, slowly at first, just how privileged I was to be able to flow back and forth between the two realms.

I was introduced by the staff to the residents as a volunteer. I told them personally that I was a sociologist, interested in learning about the hostel and the experience of living in one. At first, I felt the distance that suspicion and mistrust produce. I learned, however, that trust is easily won through kind words and a listening ear. As I grew to know the "regulars" and visitors over the months, I became a fixture at the hostel and I suspect that many forgot my stated purpose. Those with whom I had in-depth interviews were reminded, of course, but the many whom

I never managed to formally interview treated me as friend and confidante.

My study also encompassed two other settings. A housing service had been set up by the hostel to assist homeless women in finding accommodation. After I had been at the hostel for awhile, I began working at the housing service several days a week as a volunteer, in order to get exposure to the experience of "looking for a place. " In this setting, I conducted many in-depth interviews in which I provided the same information and assurances as with those held at the hostel. But, by and large, most of my time was devoted to learning about the bureaucratic problems associated with housing the poor.

The third setting was a day-time drop-in centre for transient women. This had been set up to give homeless women a place to go during the day. It was open at times when the hostels required residents to be out, and as one might expect, many of the women that I found there during the day returned to the hostel in the late afternoon or at suppertime.

The drop-in centre was of a very different character from the hostel. There were always women coming and going, and various activities going on. On my first day at the centre, the head staff person introduced me very openly and publicly as a sociologist who was studying homeless women. The women reacted blandly and seemed to be quite used to being objects of professional attention. I found, however, that because the composition of the group changed daily, it was impossible to inform all individuals who were there at any one time of my identity, as this clearly would have been interventionist. But it is the case that there were never any occasions in which most of the women there were not aware of my role, having met me before at the hostel, the housing service, or the drop-in centre.

In the chapters which follow, I will recount the observations I made about the experience of homelessness within the context of the social services. I will describe the structure of the hostel, analyze the relations between staff and residents, portray the subculture of homelessness, examine the residents' experiences of self, and suggest a critique of the downward spiral of homelessness in which the hostel has, for many, become a home.

The dilemmas of how much closeness to develop with my subjects, how much to reveal about my own life, how much to ask about their previous lives, and how much to believe, plagued me every day. The world I had the privilege to join has stayed with me since, following me like a promise made to myself never to forget. This has made it difficult to write this book, because the translation of the personal to the academic and back again is the birth process of one's reading of another culture, and requires a conscious effort to remain always "in between" the two worlds of home and away (Harman, 1987a).[2]

Notes

1. While the focus of this book is not on different strategies of providing hostels *per se*, but rather on the overall experience of homelessness among women, particularly those who spend a great deal of time in hostels, it would be unfair to simply lump the particular hostel in which the study was conducted together with all others.

   The hostel was originally formed in response to the societal and social service perception that there was no demand for shelter from women over 30 years of age. In other words, the patriarchal assumption that all "adult" women should, and would, be domesticated within the mythologized family unit prevailed, evidenced by a virtual paucity of emergency beds for women in this category. So the initial impulse for the hostel was informed by a feminist critique of the existing social services.

   Another important distinction that should be made is that the philosophy of the hostel is a collective one. This spans all levels of the organization. The board of directors and staff all work together co-operatively, with collective committees such that the board cannot override the staff. Policy and decision-making are collective as well. The work in the hostel is arranged to minimize hierarchicization. Staff and residents share cleaning and cooking tasks, unlike other hostels where cleaning staff are hired. This is done in part to minimize status differences between staff and residents, and to make the hostel feel more "homey" and less institutional.

   A final important distinction is that the philosophy of the hostel is directed toward the empowerment of women. To this end, it is totally run by women for women, and efforts are made to generate self-esteem and self-sufficiency among residents. While compared with other hostels, particularly state-run or religious-based, this hostel makes an effort to minimize the "controlling" and "infantalizing" type of institutionalization that so often characterizes hostels.

   An important question that should be asked is, if one makes a hostel "homelike", if one gives women a safe place and "all of the comforts of home", how can this be seen as bad? It is not being argued in this book that creating a domestic environment or reproducing home is necessarily bad in itself; it is rather when it becomes another context for dependency, as in the case of the chronically homeless, that there is cause for concern.

   This particular hostel is a unique alternative organization among those which exist to help the homeless. Yet it is precisely because it does not function in a vacuum, because it exists within the larger context of patriarchal ideology and patriarchal social policy, and because pressures for housing the homeless are so great, that it would be mistaken to conclude that the hostel can fully succeed in overcoming these forces.

   In this book, it will be argued that partially as a result of the strong socialization of women in our culture to feel "at home" when domesticated, and partially because of the *overall* institutionalized response of reproducing domesticity, one of the net effects, even within this particular hostel, is the reproduction of domesticity. All this said, it is very clear that the hostel workers do not believe this to be the case.

2. Where possible, I have provided verbatim excerpts from conversations and interviews. All women were guaranteed anonymity. Consequently, names and personal details have been changed to protect the rights of my subjects.

Chapter Four

The Hostel as Reproducing Domesticity: Structure and Organization

The Structure of the Hostel

The hostel under study is modeled after a "home." The physical building is a very large, old house. It is structured to resemble the typical mythologized domestic, self-contained unit, and to provide a place that transient women may, albeit temporarily, call "home." Yet, at the same time, it is tightly regulated by staff who assume a relationship over the residents that is reminiscent of a patriarchal relationship over children (*patria potestas*). The structure and organization of the hostel may be broken down into its component parts.

1. Intake

In any bureaucracy, files and records play an important role in organization and social control. Emergency hostels must keep at least minimal records so that they may report to funding agencies on the rates of use of the facilities. Records are also important in terms of the internal regulation of the hostel. With the high demand for beds and the large numbers of "hostel regulars" making repeated use of the facilities, staff maintain files on residents to aid in screening out those who are ineligible to stay.

The intake interview is the first step in this screening procedure, immediately positioning the resident-to-be as one in need of help and the staff person as one in a position to provide or deny that help. The hostel has a policy of providing shelter—space permitting—to any woman in need, as long as she meets the minimum intake requirements. These involve length of time since last stay, whether or not she has been barred in the past (a consequence of violating house rules), and general state of health.

The intake interview also ascertains the "face sheet data" of the resident-to-be, including drug and alcohol use, and criminal, psychiatric, and family violence history. Weapons are confiscated. Not infrequently, incoming residents relinquish knives; these they are entitled to take with them whenever they leave the hostel. Money and drugs are kept under lock and key in the staff room: money because otherwise it might be stolen; drugs for the protection of children and other residents in the house. Access to desirable sundries such as tobacco, aspirins, and paper products is monitored. This establishes an immediate dependency relationship between the woman and the staff, which will carry on throughout her stay. Fear of being barred from the hostel, similar to a child's fear of parental sanction, produces compliant behaviour among residents.

Residents develop techniques to manipulate staff, and staff often find themselves having to adopt a wary attitude toward residents. On the other hand, staff are also seen as knowledgeable about women's issues, housing, welfare, and employment problems. Most residents come to look up to staff as nurturing helpers who often become their friends. It is not uncommon for past residents to come back and visit the hostel for years after getting out of the condition of homelessness, and many expressed to me their deep gratitude to the staff and the hostel for having "saved" their lives.

2. Boarding Arrangements

The house is arranged with rooms of three to four beds, each bed with a dresser and chair. Women are put together somewhat randomly, due to space pressure and the need to fill vacancies as they arise. However, if violence or disruptive personal differences occur, the residents are rearranged when and as possible.

Privacy is at a minimum. Washrooms are collective. There is a large living-dining area, a TV room, kitchen, and staff room. All of these serve, at various times and in various contexts, as gathering places; however, none affords a "private place" for a woman to be alone. This is expressed in the following account:

> *Resident:* I went to bed early last night, then I was down here [in the living room] again at 2:30 a. m.
>
> *Visitor:* Why?
>
> *Resident:* Because the woman who I share with—she thinks she should have a private room—well something was bothering me and I woke up and was talking to myself. Well, she must have heard me and she told me to shut up.
>
> *Visitor:* Don't stand for that! Tell her she wouldn't listen to you so you're having a conversation with yourself! Don't stand for that! I mean it!
>
> *Resident:* Well, I told her there's no such thing as a private room [here]. Then I came down here, there were still people watching TV in the TV room! At that time! They were watching rock videos or something. Well, I finally went back up to bed at 5:30 a. m.

Another informant spoke of the kind of people she encountered in hostels:

> I've probably just run into the wrong people cause a lot of the people in hostels are, well that's mostly where I've run into people lately, well the last few years, and a lot of them have the same troubles I do, they're tired of hostels and they're totally exhausted and they just want to be left alone for a while after having to share their room with about three or four people or the whole house with like 20 or 30 people, they're just tired of looking at people some of them... Sometimes it's okay, sometimes it works out, sometimes you find nice people and you really gain from it rather than something that you just have to sort of tolerate.

3. House rules

Rules, necessary in any organization, are generated and negotiated collectively by staff. Residents are informed of the rules and the consequences of violating them. Staff exercise a great deal of discretion in their enforcement of the rules, taking individual factors into consideration and bending the rules where necessary in the best interests of the women's welfare.

i. Length of stay. Residents may stay for up to three weeks, while women with children may stay for up to four.[1] Extensions are often granted, at the discretion of the staff, particularly if there is evidence that housing will become available. Residents may also be asked to leave if they disobey house rules, or become "impossible to live with." It is assumed that the short-term emergency shelter will provide the resident with an opportunity to find work and/or a more permanent living arrangement. It is not intended as a replacement for home.

ii. Daily chore. Each woman is required to perform a daily chore. The list includes tasks such as cleaning various rooms, (living rooms, dining room, kitchen, TV room, donations room), cooking dinner, washing dishes, and taking out garbage. Each one of these chores is considered by staff to be a contribution to the operation of the hostel. Many of the women, on the other hand, define this as "work" and this gap in perception serves as a source of some conflict. One woman argued that she was being exploited and should be paid to do maid work for the hostel. Others, however, are glad for the opportunity to help, and take pride in their work. Many do much more than is asked of them. Residents routinely negotiate with staff regarding their daily chore. The following incident illustrates this type of attitude.

Researcher: How would you like to come outside and help me pick up some glass?
Resident: Where is it?
Researcher: Out on the lawn out there.
Staff: _____, have you done your chore for the day?

Resident:	Yeah, well almost.
Staff:	If you help [her] you don't have to do your chore.
Resident:	Well, I've almost finished. I just need some toilet paper for the washroom.... But what if I do the glass job [too], then do I have to do a chore tomorrow?
Staff:	No, you won't. So do you want to do it then?
Resident:	[Nods]. I just have to finish with the toilet paper, then we can go outside.

iii. No men allowed. For many residents, this rule is the key to their feeling of safety. They are safe from their troubles—troubles that more often than not are male-related. Phone calls are screened so that a resident may ask that she *not* be considered staying at the hostel as far as "so-and-so" (usually male) is concerned. These rules provide protection and anonymity. The hostel becomes a kind of fortress between the residents and a world that, for the time being at least, they would rather forget. Many of the residents voiced attitudes similar to the following:

Researcher:	Do you think you'll have a good atmosphere if you move into the [all female] group home?
Resident:	Well, I don't know. Well, for one thing there are no men. I'm safe from men.

iv. Out during the day. Between 10 a. m. and 4 p. m., all residents (with the exception of mothers with small children, and the ill) must be out of the house, ostensibly seeking work and a place to live. Toward this end, they are each provided with two subway tokens and may make a bag lunch. Many take the first streetcar to a shopping mall, park, or drop-in centre, to await the inevitable ride back for four o'clock door opening. Some women are able to find jobs and housing and only stay in this condition temporarily, but for the "chronically" homeless there often seems little point in trying. Often these women return to the hostel several hours early, wait outside and ask of staff and volunteers who approach the door, "Is it four o'clock yet?" This kind of patient "waiting" reflects the enforced idleness of homelessness. It also indicates the dependency of residents upon institutional definitions regarding when they may and may not enter the hostel, and more generally how the institution structures their sense of time.

v. In by midnight.[2] Any resident who breaks curfew without prior good reason must leave the hostel the next day. This rule establishes a certain degree of control over the activities of residents, and places a value on their beds. The staff are quite flexible in the application of this rule, and exceptions may be made for those working night shifts, or in the hospital overnight. Occasionally, the staff will grant permission for a woman to stay out all night for a social visit if she has been at the hostel for awhile. In one case, a woman pleaded that she had been rehearsing for a play and the rehearsal had gone past midnight. Fearful of traveling alone at night, she stayed with a friend.

vi. No violence, profanity or theft. Ideally, conflict is maintained at a minimum; however, as will happen in any situation of living at close quarters, violence and arguments erupt. Thefts, particularly of money and desirable items such as portable tape-recorders, are reported on a regular basis.

One informant spoke about her experiences with theft and violence in hostels, and how these led her to minimize the number of possessions that she carried with her:

> You're always losing stuff, you're afraid to have anything that's of any value, even though you can lock it up, sooner or later you end up losing it if you go around hostels a lot. The first time at [another hostel] I lost a silver and turquoise ring. The woman that was on duty said, "Maybe the person that took it needed it more than you." That's what she said to me. I couldn't believe it. And she warned me of keeping track of jeans if I had any jeans, but I didn't.

> It's just that a lot of people don't have much money and it's very hard to keep your possessions together, so the fewer you have the easier it is for you. And also to carry them around.

> Well, I was kicked, at [another hostel], and punched ... I didn't do anything ... this one woman she was crazy, she grabbed a knife and she attacked her friend ... and her friend had some martial arts, luckily for her. She still ended up in hospital.

In another case, a young woman was going through intake and the staff person noticed that her hand had been bandaged. She claimed that it had been stabbed and that she had had it looked after by a plastic surgeon. She also claimed to have stabbed a woman at another hostel.

Staff: It wasn't staff, I hope!
Resident: No, someone had gone through my things and I didn't like it. So I stabbed her.

This woman's best friend was rumoured to have been murdered on the street later that night.

4. Lock-up room

The residents may store belongings, for up to two weeks after leaving the hostel, in a large, locked room. Most place their possessions in large green garbage bags which are then labeled, denoting the resident's name and date of storage. This practice has evolved in order to give ex-residents "a break" in finding a place after leaving the hostel, for the perennial moving from hostel to hostel is stressful enough without the added burden of packing and unpacking one's earthly belongings. Among items left were clothing, furniture, luggage, bicycles. What often happens is that women who are "regulars" in the hostel circuit use the lockup as a storage depot instead of taking their accumulated possessions as they go from hostel to hostel. As a result of this practice, the staff become quite relaxed about enforcing the two-week rule and often there are bags that have been left for up to six months. When questioned, staff might say, "Oh, that's so-and-so's bag. She's at [another hostel] now, she'll be back to get her stuff sooner or later."

5. Donations Room

The "donations room" hosts scores of dresses, skirts, blouses, shoes, boots, coats, and purses that have been donated to the hostel. There is a large, full-length mirror at the end of the room and any woman may try on and take whatever items of clothing she desires. This room is of daily interest to the residents, for as new donations are brought in, sorted, and transferred to the donations room, the women compete to claim the "best" items before they are "picked over." Often they take clothes, wear them for a day or two, and return them to the room where they choose a new outfit. It is not uncommon to find nearly new, "designer" outfits donated by the well-to-do. Penniless residents are able to compile fashionable outfits with a limitless opportunity to exchange them for others, with the net result of effecting a neat, attractive appearance. One informant suggests how this resource is useful for the lifestyle of the homeless:

> It's hard sometimes to keep your stuff together. A lot of people just end up getting donations or they have donations like clothes at some of the hostels and people just take the clothes and wear them, and sometimes just wash them or put them back when they're finished with them and get more different ones.

6. Sunday Dinners

Sundays are visitors' days. From 2 o'clock on, ex-residents, residents' friends, and other women who need a hot meal are welcome to come in off the street. Dinner is usually made by the women, with a certain amount of supervision by the staff and volunteers. Games such as bingo are often played while dinner is cooking, and the TV room, dining room, and living room are usually full to overflowing. Facilities open to resident women—such as the upstairs bedrooms, donations room, and laundry room—are off-limits to visitors. Many Sunday visitors are "regulars," who are subject to rules and regulations similar to those that apply to residents. Among other things, women are asked to sign a list of chores when they arrive. Because the dinner is such a large production, often serving between sixty and one hundred women, most of the chores focus on kitchen duties such as cooking, cleaning, and doing dishes. The sanction for breaking rules entails being barred from Sunday dinners for a number of weeks or months, depending on the nature of the offence and the "past record" of the offender.

The Sunday dinners became the focus of a great deal of my observation and will be the topic of Chapter Six. They provided a regular view into the subculture of homeless women, the normative structure and systems of relevance, and the meaning that the hostel had for the women who were residents or who had been residents in the past. They also provided a context in which I became a regular member, allowing me to develop trusting bonds with many women and affording opportunities to engage in follow-up interviews later on in the week.[3]

The Drop-in Centre

At the drop-in centre, transient women "recreate" during the day. There are two large rooms with tables, chairs, and sofas. Women have access to a free telephone, a newspaper, a television that generally stays tuned to soap operas, decks of cards, knitting needles, crochet hooks, and scrap yarn. The main attraction, however, is the "makeover" by a staff person. This service is offered free of charge and may entail a haircut and set, facial makeup and manicure. The staff are generally able to "work miracles" and vastly improve the appearance, and hence temporarily the self-image, of the women in question. There is also a small donations corner where clothes are available for free, as well as a bottomless cup of coffee and a daily soup lunch.

Various activities such as swimming and bowling are organized, along with an occasional dance. When asked by the researcher why lifestyle skills were not offered, a staff person answered, "We tried that before. They would rather have their nails done."[4]

The Housing Office

The mandate of the housing office was to facilitate the transition of women from the hostel to their own, independent living arrangements. To this end, staff developed listings of housing affordable to welfare recipients; counseled the women who came to their office; contacted the welfare office if necessary in order to secure advance "emergency" funds to cover first and last months' rent (money that the women could rarely come up with on their own and would have to repay out of subsequent welfare cheques); and often accompanied the women to prospective residences.[5]

I spent time assisting staff and performing consultations. In an overwhelming number of cases, the only "affordable" housing was a room in a rooming house. Clients complained of absentee landlords, cockroach and lice infestations, faulty locks, lack of heat, violent and noisy neighbours. The following accounts of living in a rooming house are typical:

> You can hear everything and see the lights on in other peoples' places. There's no privacy. It's a rooming house and he's [landlord] doing this without a licence. That's illegal. He claims it doesn't come under the landlord/tenant act. The building inspector has been around and urged us to band together and hold our rent until he does what he has said. Ha! With that bunch? No one cares. There are fights in the halls, people smoking pot, playing rock music which bothers me a lot. They can have their pot if they would only turn down the music. It's a weird bunch. There's only one other person who's quiet. The others are just glad to have a place to stay. The landlord doesn't object to wild parties and all that. He even calls the immigration office to get tenants—probably refugees—it's a landlord's market. I just stopped telling the landlord about all the problems because he wasn't listening.

Informant:	You know, I am so afraid where I live, I don't even have a chain on the door, just a lock and anyone can get in with a key, it is so easy.
Researcher:	Why don't you put on a chain?
Informant:	Well, I hope to be leaving there soon.
Researcher:	Then you can take it with you.
Informant:	She'd [the landlady] never let me. You know there was a chain there before and she broke it. I was asleep and she tried to get in and pushed and pushed on the door until it broke. Then she blamed me, she said I did it on purpose. What can I do? I was asleep.

In general, the type of housing available engendered a feeling of fear and apprehension of being "a single woman out there." Many of the women who were placed in such housing turned up weeks later at the hostel and/or drop-in centre: recidivists to the hostel circuit.

Conclusion

From the structure and organization of the social services provided for homeless women, it is evident that there is an effort to emulate the private domain of home, both in the physical arrangement of the house and in the set of roles that women are expected to play. Homeless women are sheltered, made "homeful," in a way which makes them invisible to the public eye. As the saying goes, "out of sight, out of mind." But what transpires within the home, behind the walls which hide? What are the interpersonal processes by which the hostel becomes a home?

Notes

1. At the time the study was conducted, these stays were shorter by one week. The hostel policy was changed in response to the growing housing crisis in the city. Another recent change is the introduction of an open-door policy allowing women with children who are on a waiting list for subsidized housing to stay at the shelter until their housing becomes available, usually for two to six months.

2. Since the study was conducted, this rule was revised to allow residents to stay out until 2 a.m. on weekends.

3. Methodologically, the existence of this group and my ability to meet with it regularly was an ethnographer's dream come true. It made it possible for me to develop friendships and trusting relationships with my subjects, and to develop more than a superficial understanding of the subculture. For these reasons, the bulk of my findings derive from my exposure to this group.

   It is important to stress that the "Sunday regulars" are not representative of all women who make use of the hostel. They have evolved into a clique and tend to dominate the hostel on Sundays. In fact, many residents find it upsetting to have the hostel transformed so dramatically on Sundays, often staying in their rooms or making a point of leaving for the day.

   The information derived from by observations and interviews, then, is somewhat one-sided. I did not stay in the hostel 24 hours a day every day of the week, nor did I have many opportunities to observe one-on-one interactions between staff and residents, interactions which may have shown a different side of things. The day-to-day operations of the hostel may have shed more light on ways in which hostel workers become friends and "family" for the women staying at the hostel; ways in which they helped them, such as taking them to hospital, helping them move, helping them find a place, recommending them for new housing initiatives, et cetera. I heard about many such events in the "folklore" of the regulars, as they related their own gratitude to the hostel workers for all of the things they had done for them.

4. It is worth noting that this drop-in centre does not share the same feminist philosophy of empowerment as the hostel, but rather more closely approximates the spirit of *parens patriae*.

5. As noted above, this practice is no longer possible for female clients.

Chapter Five

Staff, Power, and Relations of Control

Relations Between Staff and Residents
Relations between staff and residents reflect the legitimacy of control accorded to imputational specialists within the system of *parens patriae*.[1] There is a self-fulfilling prophecy entailed in the provision of emergency shelter which makes such relations necessary, although most who work in the system would agree that they are not necessarily desirable.

The relations between staff and residents observed within the hostel must be understood within the larger context of homelessness among women, and the structural constraints around the provision of emergency shelter. The staff at this hostel are recruited with a major qualification being a commitment to feminism and the empowerment of women. The staff evidenced a deep concern for the health and wellbeing of the residents, and a strong belief that they were doing something important. Nevertheless, the contradictions entailed in working in the hostel are sometimes oppressive and may result in a hardening of attitudes. As one staff person put it,

> When I first got my degree, I thought I would go out and change the world. As a strong feminist, I really wanted to help battered women. But I now realize that I can't help them at all. In this job the most I can do is to put on a bandaid and send them back out into the world.

How does this hardening come about? In the first place, there are simply not enough resources to meet all of the needs of homeless women. Resources in this case include the human resources of attention, supervision, and control, and the material resources of food, shelter, and clothing. Such resources are scarce and must be charily distributed. Second, because of funding structures, hostels are required to be tightly regulated. This positions the staff in roles that, in practice, tend to be closer to those of police than care-givers. Third, because of the brevity of the stay at the hostel, staff have only limited contact with the women and can not always have the kind of long-term impact that they would like.

Finally, because of the open-door policy of this particular hostel, there is a colourful mixture of clientele. The subculture of homelessness, particularly among the chronically homeless, is one in which "street smarts" are essential to survival. Experienced staff find it necessary to be wary of the possibility of theft, profanity, violence, deceit, and manipulation of authority figures.

From the perspective of residents, the staff have the power of denying them a home. This is a great power, one that residents fear having turned against them. Residents see the staff as both enemy and saviour, and the tension between these two roles is expressed in the ways in which residents find to manipulate staff to achieve desired outcomes. Staff are the guardians of the home, the gatekeepers to the scarce resource of the shelter. They hold the keys, both literally and figuratively, to domesticity, no matter how temporary.

Much of the time, both staff and residents were mistrustful of each other. There were frequent accusations of lying, and others were often called upon to verify statements. As one would expect, such strategies served to further polarize the positions of staff versus residents, while offering incentives to some members, particularly among the residents, to "squeal" on the others. Conflicts and negotiations between staff and residents centred on the continual effort on the part of residents to "get more" out of the staff in terms of scarce commodities such as food, tokens, bingo prizes, and tobacco. This produced an environment wherein residents attempted to get on the "good side" of staff, to get beyond the mistrust, so that they might have access to scarce resources and relaxed rules. One outcome of this environment was the development of a hierarchy among residents and regulars, wherein certain members were seen to have "negotiating power" or "pull" when interacting with staff. Another outcome was the development of certain privileged roles, particularly in the kitchen on Sundays. Finally, staff were evaluated on the basis of how strictly or rigidly they imposed rules, and whether or not they could be manipulated in the perennial struggle to "get more."

A Dramaturgical Analysis

The relations between residents and staff unfolded unexpectedly before my eyes as the most fascinating component of hostel life. I found myself in a setting in which sides were taken, strategies planned, and performances enacted. Goffman's (1959) dramaturgical model of analysis is very useful in understanding the way in which space was appropriated and scenes were acted out within the hostel.

Goffman argues that reality is socially constructed through a series of performances, which require actors, scripts, audience, front regions, and back regions. Front region denotes the public arena in which the script is enacted, in which roles are played out. Back region, on the other hand, describes the private world of preparation, retreat, and adjustment of the self to the script.

Life in the hostel revealed itself to be a series of performances, often pitting staff against residents, with a fairly fluid transition between front and back regions. The house was divided into staff territory (staff room and locked rooms) and resident territory (kitchen and other house rooms as required), which at various times served as front and back regions.

In my marginal role as volunteer, I was privy to front and back regions of both groups. From the perspective of the staff, I was seen to have access to the secrets and activities of the residents. Much of the staff room conversation revolved around residents. Initially, I did most of the asking, but I eventually came to be perceived as somewhat of an insider, in that, as the study progressed, I had probed the world of the hostel women considerably. About halfway through the year, one staff member went so far as to say to me, "Lesley, you've reached these women more than we ever could. We simply don't have the time, or the resources, to enable us to get so close." Despite my promise not to reveal any information given to me in confidence, on occasion I would be approached by a staff member for information regarding a particular resident (which of course I refused). Thus, in the back region of the staff room, I was perceived as a partial member as well as an informant. Goffman (1963b) might say that I was "wise" to the world of the staff, but due to my marginality I could never be part of the "own."[2]

From the perspective of the residents and regulars, I also became "wise." For them, my marginality meant that I had a certain amount of control without authority. The control was provided by the set of keys I carried, allowing access to locked rooms and their contents. The authority for any disciplinary decisions, however, rested with the staff alone. As I was not staff, I was not "the potential enemy," yet I was one whose affiliations might produce beneficial results. Residents often confided their strategies to me. I was seen to be a route to the staff, someone who might be sent to represent the residents in requests for certain special considerations. This was felt most when I was involved in the kitchen on Sundays, and in my role as "caller" for bingo games. I was also "wise" because I demonstrated a clear interest in the welfare of the women, often inquiring about their housing situations and on several occasions assisting them, through the housing office, with finding accommodation. Those with whom I held in-depth interviews came to trust me, and to count on my memory of the details of their accounts. This, as it turned out, was a rare kind of attention in their world. Just having someone who listened with interest and compassion, and remembered them as different from someone else, was both unusual and highly valued.

An Effort to "Get More"

The staff were generally, and incorrectly, perceived to have access to unlimited quantities of desirable commodities, and residents utilized any opportunity to attempt to "get more". This unfortunate state of affairs made it necessary for staff to impose even more stringent controls upon their resources. This situation resulted in a contradiction between the genuine desire for the charitable provision for the poor, and the necessity of rationing and frequent denial when true "need" could not be demonstrated. The types of commodities viewed as desirable included food, tokens, bingo prizes, and tobacco. Although clothing did not quite fall into the same category as the above because it was always available in large quantities, the scarcity of *desirable* clothing produced certain conflicts that should be reported.

1. Food.

There were four areas of the house in which food was kept. In the kitchen, the refrigerator contained prepared food, leftovers, milk, and perishables. Any resident or visitor was welcome to help herself to the refrigerator. Kitchen shelves and cupboards contained the bulk dry ingredients used in cooking, such as flour, sugar, herbs, and spices, and again were open to general access. There was one locked cupboard, in which were kept small quantities of foodstuffs over which control was exercised. These included coffee, chocolate, and canned goods. The main food storage room, which was kept locked, was in the basement. Butter, bread, vegetables, and meat were kept frozen. There were three walls of shelving in which canned goods and bulk dried goods were stored.

Because of the expense, limited supply, desirability, and easy portability of foods that were locked up, they were only available through the gatekeeper of staff or volunteer. Residents developed various strategies for "getting more" food. On Sundays, for example, the kitchen regulars created needs that would call for certain highly desirable ingredients. One favorite way to do this was dreaming up dessert recipes. "Chocolate chocolate chip" cookies were a real treat, and they required large quantities of butter and chocolate, and usually a special trip to the store to buy chocolate chips.

By securing the permission of the staff to make a particular dish, the residents could justify "getting more" of certain highly desirable ingredients. The experience of being able to actually spend money in the public domain on highly valued consumer items became an end in itself, and one that was otherwise rare in the lives of these women.

"Getting more" food also involved certain activities connected with Sunday dinners (these will be reported in more detail in Chapter Six). Women working in the kitchen would set aside choice portions of dinner for themselves and their friends before letting in the line of hungry women. On occasion, I observed these women slyly wrapping up pieces of meat or dessert in paper towels or foil, and slipping them into their bags. The kitchen, as a "back region" in the short time before dinner when its doors were closed, served as a context for such actions that were understood to be legitimate by the women practising them because they had "earned it" through their efforts in preparing the meal.

Finally, "getting more" food on Sundays was attempted by the women in line as they were served by the kitchen regulars. The servers had to make the food stretch for large numbers of people, so generally gave small portions to each, with the promise of second helpings if there was enough to go around. Some women, however, pleaded for more. Being hungry, an almost universal state among the homeless, was not in itself a good enough reason for more food. Being a special friend of the kitchen regulars got one an extra-large helping, as did being staff or a volunteer. Being sick or pregnant was seen as legitimate, and children and teenagers were considered to be growing, thus needy.

2. Tokens.

Part of the subsistence services included the provision of subway tokens so that the women staying in the hostel could come and go during the day. But it was "public" knowledge that these tokens were kept in the office, and often residents would ask for additional tokens, assuming boundless quantities. Visitors also assailed staff with requests for tokens, even though they "knew" that tokens were only made available to residents. In both cases, there was a systematic effort to appear exceptional so that existing rules could be bent. On the part of the staff, there was a sense of exasperation at having to clamp down so hard by systematically denying any exceptions. Subway tokens, so trivial in the larger scheme of things, took on high value as a scarce commodity.

3. Bingo Prizes.

During the winter, a favourite weekly activity was playing bingo. It helped to "pass the time," and there was a chance that one would win a prize. Sundays, I assumed the role of "caller" for the bingo games, and so was exposed to the strategy of "getting more" bingo prizes.

The hostel had a storage room where donations of Christmas presents and miscellaneous gifts were kept. Even though many women attended the annual Christmas party where gifts were given out, there were usually quite a few left over. These served as the pool of bingo prizes. Some were wrapped, so that their contents could not be detected, while others were not wrapped. They tended to be small, inexpensive items that fell into the categories of personal grooming items, clothing accessories, and costume jewellery. Under personal grooming items would be included soap, perfume, makeup, combs, shampoo and conditioner, nail polish, lipstick, foundation, and bath products. Under clothing accessories would be items like stockings and underwear. Under jewellery would be earrings, rings, and necklaces. There were occasionally other, larger items (such as a lamp or a board game), but these were quite exceptional.

There was a clear hierarchy of desirable prizes, whereby items that were the most useful to the women were the most highly valued. Everyday items that were defined as "necessities," such as shampoo, soap, and stockings would be put to use and would not, then have to be purchased, therefore constituting a savings. Next, items that were defined as "luxuries," such as costume jewellery, perfume, and bath products, were valued. Items that could not really be of use were the least desirable. The lamp presents a case in point. The item itself was attractive by prevailing standards of aesthetics, and would have commanded a high price in the retail market. However, the woman who won it in the bingo game responded by saying, "Great, a lamp! What's someone like me going to do with a lamp? I don't even have a place to stay."

The responsibility for setting up the bingo game usually fell on my shoulders. After dinner was in the oven, there was often a period of an hour or two to "kill" before it was time to eat. Usually Daisy, one of the Sunday regulars, would remind me that it was time to get the bingo set up, and that I should round up some prizes. I would then go to the staff room and inquire as to whether it would be all right to take some prizes from the storage room. Until the prizes were depleted in about March, I was permitted to take about six items each week. I would then go down to the basement meeting room where the bingo was played, unlock the room, and spread the prizes out on the table. Daisy usually accompanied me to monitor the prizes. She would pronounce her judgment as to whether or not there were enough, whether they were "good enough," and I would invariably be entreated to get more. However, at this point I always had to act as intermediary between the women and the staff, saying "no," invoking scarcity as the rule. Daisy's assessment of whether the prizes were good enough clearly reflected the hierarchy outlined above. On one occasion, I had brought down a handful of cheap rings in addition to a number of small wrapped packages. She announced that no one would want the rings, and indeed when it came to awarding the prizes they were the last to go.

Setting up also included calling through the house that bingo was about to begin, so that any interested women would be informed, and setting up the table with the cards, chips for covering numbers, and the cage from which the numbers were drawn.

When all of the women who wanted to play bingo were seated, Daisy would usually announce what prizes there were, and there would be some brief discussion about them before the game actually began. Consensus on the value of the prizes was easily reached, establishing a competitive environment wherein whoever won first would have her pick. Wrapped prizes were handled, shaken, and smelled to ascertain their contents. When the contents were not obvious, the women would usually opt for the most desirable unwrapped items before taking a gamble on wrapped items.

By taking the role of the caller, I freed everyone else to play, which was appreciated. However, the person who regularly took charge of the bingo game was Daisy. She kept an eagle eye over everyone else's cards, as well as her own, to make sure that everyone got the numbers that were called. When someone cried "Bingo," Daisy would rush over to make sure that, in fact, she had won fairly. She would then make suggestions as to which prize the winner should pick, even though it was up to the individual to decide. Usually, the prize was passed around the table so that everyone could take a look at it, especially if the woman had to unwrap it and its contents were a surprise. As the game progressed, the pool of desirable prizes was depleted, and women might even elect not to take an undesirable prize. In the case of the rings, by the end of the game there were still several left on the table.

There was an underlying sense of fair play that made the bingo more co-operative than competitive. It was felt that everyone should have a chance to win a prize, and if someone won more than one, there was subtle pressure to give the extras to women who had not won. It was fascinating to watch how these women, who had nothing, were generous with the gifts that had been provided by the hostel. One regular routinely gave away her prizes unless she had immediate use for them. She once gave me some bath salts, saying, "Oh, Lesley, you probably can make better use of these than I can. I don't want to carry them around!"

The final stage of valuation of the prizes occurred when the game was over and the women made their way back upstairs to help in the final stages of preparation for dinner. Those who had not played were curious about the prizes won, and those who had played proudly displayed their winnings.

4. Tobacco.

Smoking is a popular pastime among homeless women. Most of the women utilizing the services of the hostel smoked, and the importance of smoking is highlighted by one non-smoker's comment that, "I don't smoke, so I don't have anything to do in the evening."[3]

Cigarettes are expensive. For a heavy smoker, the cost of cigarettes can easily outweigh that of food. For the poor, smoking often occupies the contradictory status of being both a luxury and a necessity. It is a luxury in that smokers may forego other "necessities" for their cigarettes. It is a necessity precisely because it occupies a position alongside of housing, food, and clothing as an essential of subsistence living.

The hostel stocked cans of tobacco, which were offered in limited quantities to residents and visitors. Usually on Sundays the staff were cautious with how much they put out because, being a highly portable and highly valuable commodity, it "disappears" quickly. Smokers regularly attempted to "get more" tobacco from the staff room by appearing at the door and claiming that the tobacco was all gone. While it was usually the case that there was none left, the staff maintained a high level of suspicion as to the destination of the tobacco, and were reluctant to put out more than one can per Sunday. Residents provided a variety of justifications for putting out more, including "I didn't get any—those residents took it all. That's no fair, they're no poorer than we are. We do all these chores, and for nothing, not even a smoke!" or "There wasn't a whole can in the first place, and I didn't get a chance to get any," or a favourite, "I know you have lots of tobacco. Can't you just spare one more can?"

Attempts at "getting more" tobacco were directed toward others within the subculture as well as toward staff. Tactics ranged from theft, to "bumming," to collecting old butts. Cigarettes were regularly reported as having been "stolen," and many vicious arguments erupted when one woman accused another of having stolen her cigarettes. Staff, again with the presumption of dishonesty foremost in their interpretation of these situations, often questioned whether the accusor had even had any cigarettes to lose.

"Bumming" was regularly practised and served as a basis for establishing insider and outsider status. Close friends shared cigarettes generously, and seemed to keep a mental tab on "who owed what." As long as the debts were more or less reciprocated on a regular basis, there was little reluctance to share what they had. Outsiders and those who had been defined as non-reciprocating, on the other hand, were summarily refused cigarettes, such refusal usually being accompanied by some kind of put-down.

Collecting butts was generally regarded as a desperate move. It involved retrieving used butts from ashtrays, removing the remaining tobacco, and using that tobacco to roll a new cigarette. Whether one was forced to use this option, or used hostel tobacco, or brought one's own store-bought cigarettes, became a kind of statement regarding one's degree of poverty. On one Sunday, as the kitchen regulars sat around the table after dinner smoking cigarettes and drinking coffee, one woman began to empty butts that she had collected onto the table. As the others watched, it became apparent that most of the regulars who were on welfare had brought their own store-bought packs, which sat on the table beside their coffee cups. One woman in this category said, "Wow, you must really be poor if you have to do that." Another agreed, proudly saying, "I would never do that. I always buy mine."

One chain-smoking informant, a proud woman who, despite her destitution, still thought of herself as "middle-class," revealed her own strategy for "managing" the fact that she simply could not afford to buy the number of cigarettes that she smoked each day. She removed from her purse a perfect cardboard cigarette package, and opened it to reveal a collection of butts. "I'm sorry," she apologised to me, "I'm reduced to smoking butts," and gratefully smoked about five of my own store-bought cigarettes during the remainder of the interview.

5. Desirable Clothing.

Quantities of clothing are never lacking. If anything, the hostel receives more donations than it has room or demand for. Donations from philanthropic citizens arrive almost daily, and one of the more tedious chores of the staff and volunteers is sorting through the clothing before it is made available to residents. There are three categories used in determining the destination of the donations: donations room; hostel use; and Goodwill.[4] Items in the first two categories are considered to be of use to residents; those in the third are sent on to Goodwill.

What were the criteria staff used for "usefulness"? First, the clothing must be sturdy, clean, and practical. As one staff member put it, "Homeless women have no use for satin evening gowns." Items that would serve to protect the women from the elements, such as leather boots, coats, hats, sweaters, and slacks, were particularly desirable. Second, there was a kind of aesthetic used in the selecting of clothing that would conform to a middle-class notion of "good taste." This was one way in which staff reproduced their own standards of decorum. On several occasions when going through donations, staff would hold up an item of clothing, make a face and refer to it as "hideous" or "in bad taste". Preferences were for natural materials, such as cotton, wool, linen, and leather, while synthetics were often discarded.

A great deal of the donated clothing fell into the categories of "useless" or "in bad taste." In part this may be because people donating clothing that they do not wear may use similar criteria in selecting which clothing to discard. Most of this was sent on to Goodwill. The clothing that was kept was divided into two groups. The clothing for general hostel use included lingerie, which was kept in a hall closet with the bedding and made available to residents upon demand, and mittens, gloves and hats, which were kept in the staff room and given out freely to residents and visitors who needed them. The remaining clothing was destined for the donations room. Depending on its size and "desirability," it might be snatched up quickly, or sit in the room for months without being used.

Because of the diversity in ages, class backgrounds, and therefore the "tastes" of the women utilizing the hostel, it is difficult to generalize as to what constituted desirable clothing. Teenagers went after clothing that was fashionable for their age group, while older women tended to seek more conservative items. It is safe to say, however, that most of the women were very concerned with their appearance. Part of the goal was to "look nice," to rise, in a sense, above the level of destitution they had reached through their homelessness. Another part of the goal was to "look feminine," and this applied to other aspects of appearance as well, including hair and makeup.

This use of clothing, reminiscent of "expressive role supportive" behaviour, was highlighted on occasions when I was sorting through bags of donations. When there had been a very large influx of donations—including food, plates, and cutlery for the kitchen—the sorting of the clothing might have to be done out in the hall while other sorting took place in the staff room. This was not an efficient context for performing the task. In the staff room, as a back region, one could consult with the staff and make decisions about the clothing without having the residents interfere, enabling sorting to be done relatively efficiently. Curious residents would often poke their heads into the staff room and ask, "What is there?" or "Oh, can I have that?" but it was easy enough to close the door or tell them to wait until we had finished sorting.

In the front region of the hallway, there was nothing to prevent the residents from tearing into the boxes and bags, making a mess of the piles that the sorter had made, and making off with clothing that may or may not have been destined for the hostel. The excitement of receiving a new shipment of donations can be likened to that of a sale at Creeds.[5] On several occasions I was literally mobbed as I tried to sort the clothing in public, and when the "crowds" subsided, all of the bags would be in disarray, with clothing strewn all over the floor. Women would fight over "choice" items of clothing, the victors gleefully rushing up to their rooms to try on their new acquisitions. One time, a woman was checking out of the hostel and had left her green garbage bag full of clothing in the hallway, by the door to the staff room. A large shipment of donations arrived, consisting of six large green garbage bags. A mob scene ensued, only after which it became apparent that the residents had opened the departing woman's bag and taken some of her own clothing. When I asked her to check what was missing, she seemed nonchalant and said, "Oh, it doesn't really matter. I can always get more."

What were the kinds of clothing that the women fought over? They generally conformed to the categories used by staff to sort through the donations, although one criterion was quite apparent in the exclamations of the residents: that the clothing be either new or nearly new. New clothing was distinguishable because it would have the original tags or wrapping on it, while nearly new clothing appeared to have been worn once or twice at the most. It was not uncommon to receive quite a few items in this condition, and they were often the first to be snatched up. As one woman confided to me:

> I finally decided to take a look in the donations room—I'd never been down there before—they have some really nice clothes, some new ones with the tags still on [she points to her blouse]. This one still had a tag on and it's nice. And this [blue corduroy] jacket is nice, and these [peach] pants don't look like they've ever been worn.

Feminine lingerie was also a very popular item. Delicate underwear, or fine nightwear, went quickly. Once a pale blue and beige lace camisole with matching panties was donated. The size was quite petite. As the throng of curious residents gathered around me, a very heavy woman grabbed the set and stood there, running her hands over it and murmuring, "So soft, so beautiful, I wonder if it will fit me?" I looked at her and said, "No, I doubt it!" She held it up to her body and said, "You're probably right, but I want to keep it just the same. It makes me feel so feminine just to know I have it," and ran up to her room. On another occasion, I remarked to a resident who was wearing a brightly flowered housecoat, "Don't you look pretty today! Is that new?" and she answered, "Yes, it just came in today. I was lucky to get it."

To the poor, clothing is a luxury that they can rarely afford to buy new. But those who do buy new clothing are quick to let the others know. One wintry Sunday, a regular appeared at the hostel. Instead of taking off her coat and boots, she paraded around the living room fully attired, making sure that her friends noticed. One woman observed, "That looks like a new purse and boots you have on there. Where did you get them, the donations room?" The woman proudly exclaimed, "No, I bought them. At Woolworth's. Upstairs, not down in the basement where you get the cheap stuff." Approving murmurs were heard throughout the room, and women approached her and asked if they could touch her purse.

Notes

1. It should be noted that many of the observations which follow could be generalized to the "helping professions" will refer to current, past and potential residents, while the term "regulars" will refer to those who made up the subculture of homelessness. Many of the observations made occurred at Sunday dinners, where the "subculture of homelessness" emerged, and the generalizations may not apply to all women who were using the services of the hostel.

2 In Goffman's book *Stigma: Notes on the Management of Spoiled Identity*
   (1963b), he advanced our understanding of the nature of deviant subcultures and the ways in which others relate to them. His distinction between
   the "own" and the "wise" was basically that between "one of us" and
   "someone who is not quite one of us but understands us, how we are
   different, what our needs are." So, in the helping professions those
   practitioners who become confidantes of members of deviant subcultures
   may be the "wise." In the context of this study, I became "wise" to both the
   homeless subculture and the staff, at the same time that I could never be
   part of the "own."

3. Since the study was conducted, there have been some non-smoking areas
   instituted in the hostel.

4. The Goodwill is a charitable organization which received donations and
   sells them at their low-cost retail outlets.

5. Creeds, an exclusive ladies' fashion store in Toronto, is known for its mark-
   down sales at which otherwise self-respecting citizens form mobs in an
   effort to get the best bargains.

Chapter Six:

Going Home For Sunday Dinner:
The Subculture of Homelessness

Sunday dinners constitute a weekly enactment of the domestic ritual, and form the centre around which revolves the subculture of homelessness. Here we find most of the ingredients of the mythologized home packaged within another myth: that of the "Sunday dinner".

The myth of the Sunday dinner entails the gathering of the extended family for a weekly feast and family reunion on the culturally defined "day of leisure," within the context of the domestic unit. The gendered division of labour is typically played out with women in the kitchen and the men and children they serve enjoying Sunday leisure activities. Within this myth is contained the structure which supports the cultural norm of Sunday as a day of leisure. It is clearly not a day of leisure for all; in fact, in order for the world of paid labour to have the day "off," focus shifts to the unpaid domestic worker to provide and organize leisure and consumption activities for family members.

This occasion for "playing house" can be understood through the application of Goffman's dramaturgical model. For Goffman, much of everyday life is dedicated to the "management" of interaction to produce a consistent presentation of self. Consistency is expected, as roles offer ready-made scripts for individuals to enact. In turn, others' behaviour can be readily predicted on the basis of their assumption of scripted roles. At the level of culture, role sets provide a kind of predictability which is necessary in navigating a world of strangers (Harman, 1987a). Private and public worlds are linked through the re-enactment, again and again, of culturally scripted plays. The performance of Sunday dinner is just one ritual play that is definitive of our patriarchal culture. Through its analysis, we can recognize the gendered division of labour at the level of everyday life. We will then turn to the Sunday dinner as it is enacted in the hostel, with an eye to patterns and similarities between the public and the private dimensions of the ritual.

The woman occupying the role of "expressive superior" must play stage manager for this performance of leisure. Her complex set of unpaid duties—which Rosenberg (1986) has termed "housework," "mother-work," and "wifework,"—entails a delicate balance between the front and back regions of the domestic unit. Within the home, certain areas are "on display," or front regions, when the performance of Sunday dinner is being staged. These include rooms of the house that are to be used during the ritual, such as the living room, dining room, main floor washroom, and playroom if children are among the visitors. Most of these rooms will be on the main floor and will be prepared as public regions for the reception of the scrutinizing audience/co-actors. Prior to and after the performance, they may constitute "back regions" in preparation for, and in conclusion of, the event. These regions are seen as exemplary of a host of traits, including neatness and decorative flair, which are usually attributed to the expressive superior. In turn, they also represent the socioeconomic status of the "breadwinner" by signifying— through the value of the furnishings, electronic gadgetry and other consumer items—the breadwinner's disposable income. Other areas, such as the upstairs rooms (bedrooms, second bathrooms, studies) are back regions throughout. And some areas, which remain back regions during the performance, are turned into front regions afterwards (for example, the kitchen, when as is often done, women visitors move in to help with the cleaning up after the meal).

The duties of the stage manager include (1) planning the menu and shopping for food and various props (flowers, table decorations); (2) preparing food, sometimes, as with baking, beginning days ahead; (3) setting the domestic stage to receive visitors (extended family members and friends) who may serve as actors and audience in turn; (4) "managing" the performance (balancing front and back regions, which is epitomized by running back and forth between the kitchen and the dining room, or the kitchen and the living room); and finally, when it is all over, (5) cleaning up the set (doing dishes, dealing with leftovers, cleaning the house again).

The Sunday dinner, then, is not a casual event that "just happens." It is a culturally scripted performance, the success of which rests largely on the talents of the stage manager. Yet its enduring place as a cultural icon is of importance when seeking to understand the prevailing hegemony of family patriarchy. The Sunday dinner is a central mechanism in reaffirming the family in a world which threatens to tear it apart.

Sunday Dinner at the Hostel

Sunday dinner at the hostel is an important regular event in the lives of many women, for whom participating in the dinner fulfills more than the simple function of being fed. Sunday dinner is a ritual, played out in a manner similar to that of the iconographic Sunday dinner described above.

At two o'clock on Sunday afternoons, the hostel opens its doors to any women who wish to visit. Regulars on the hostel circuit know of this, as do former residents who have managed to find housing and income, perhaps even employment. The visitors vary from week to week, both in their numbers and in their personal situations. The size of the gathering is affected by factors like (1) the weather—if it is very cold and snowy out, the hostel is likely to be an attractive place to go, while on warm summer days the numbers dwindle—and (2) holidays—Christmas and Thanksgiving are very popular times, for there is always plenty of turkey and "holiday" food, perhaps gifts, and certainly plenty of company.

The group is composed of several subgroups, all of whom play vital functions in the Sunday dinner performance. First, the current residents at the hostel usually eat with the visitors. Residents are in a special category because they have access to all parts of the house regularly open to them, while the visitors are permitted to stay in certain sections only. Second, the "Sunday regulars" form a tight clique of friends for whom Sunday dinners are a regular social event. They are pivotal in putting on the show, in that, collectively, they assume the role of "expressive superiors." Finally, there is a third category of "visitors," which may include occasional regulars, women staying in other hostels, or visitors of women staying in the hostel. They play a more peripheral role, but give the "regulars" their centrality. In addition to the clientele, the two other important sets of actors are the staff and volunteers.

It is important to note that all of the women share a common condition of defining themselves, or having defined themselves in the past, as homeless. They constitute a community that organizes itself around the institution of Sunday dinner at the hostel. Like all communities, this community has its own normative order, boundaries determining insiders from outsiders, a status hierarchy, a language, and a code of honour. The subculture of homelessness has at its centre the Sunday dinners at the hostel; it depends on these for its existence and it derives its identity from the combination of dependency and domesticity that is engendered by this institutional arrangement.

Numbers in the house for Sunday dinner can climb to sixty or more, and the "intimate" atmosphere of the day-to-day living arrangements is routinely disrupted. All accessible space is generally full, and while there is often a great deal of friendly comraderie, there are also frequent disputes, with theft and violence erupting now and then. The social control of the staff and the volunteers is omnipresent, as potential if not real in its effect. The threat of being barred from Sunday dinners is a strong deterrent to any "deviant" behaviour, and also serves as a motivator for the "regulars" to police the other "visitors" in the interests of minimizing problems.

The Kitchen

Within our culture, the kitchen is defined as the "woman's room" of the domestic unit. Not only is it her prison, trapping and isolating her within the private realm, but the kitchen is the one room in which woman is seen, and expected, to have control. The order and condition of the kitchen are seen to be a woman's responsibility, as are the process and the products of woman's kitchen labour. It is a stage that is primarily controlled by women, in that the props, process, and the actors entering and leaving are determined by women. Husbands and children are fed there daily, enjoined to stay and help clean up, and shooed out when they are defined as interfering with kitchen activities such as baking or floor washing. Friends are invited in for coffee in the mythologized "coffee klatch," a women's institution whereby the kitchen serves as a context for sharing experiences, consciousness raising, and empowerment. Men are typically made to feel like intruders in that realm, and kept ignorant of the kitchen's mechanisms through the omnipresent control of the woman. Indeed, men wishing to equalize domestic labour are placed in a position of rewriting the scripts; they must learn from women how to "use" kitchen implements—like dishwashers and microwaves—and must learn to feel comfortable in the kitchen, which entails knowing "where things go" (Luxton, 1986).

On Sundays, the kitchen in the hostel serves many of the same functions as the kitchen in the ideal typical domestic unit. It is the central gathering place, with coffee, tea, and cigarettes serving as "social lubricators," facilitating interaction. It becomes the territory of the women, not the staff; thus the staff, like men in the domestic unit, are seen as "intruders" when they enter.

For women who have no home, the lack of a kitchen, with all of the associations of woman's power that go along with it, is strongly felt. The women gravitate to the kitchen and derive great comfort from its familiar surroundings. This is built into the structure and organization of the hostel, for many of the women's daily chores—such as cooking, doing dishes, cleaning, and taking out the garbage—involve kitchen duties.

Cooking is a particularly empowering activity. It entails a degree of autonomy rarely allowed for in the world of the homeless. The regulars usually prefer to do the cooking themselves, although during the week the staff and volunteers often supervise or take an active role in the preparation of meals. On Sundays, however, the kitchen is controlled by the women. Staff inform the kitchen regulars what there is to cook, in the form of a main protein dish and vegetables, but the women decide how they are going to prepare the food, what type of salad to make, and what dessert will be served. Since large quantities of food must be prepared, these decisions are limited by the quantities of ingredients on hand, and must be approved by a staff person. After that, most of the preparation is done by the women themselves, with the help of a volunteer who provides access to the food storage areas. Indeed, the bulk of the control is in the hands of the regulars, and the menu planning, food preparation, and the serving of food becomes a source of status. Food itself is used as a source of reward and punishment.

The Sunday dinners at the hostel dramatize quite profoundly how domesticity is reproduced. This can be seen by highlighting parallels with the performance of the ideal typical Sunday dinner. First, we must establish the various role sets, and then we may proceed to analyze the various scenes of the performance. In the domestic unit we may identify (1) instrumental superior (patriarch), (2) expressive superior (matriarch), (3) children, (4) extended family, and (5) other visitors. In Goffman's language, we can say that the domestic unit acts as a "team," sustaining a definition of the situation and consistent presentation of self. The expressive superior serves as "stage manager," while the extended family and visitors can be both part of the team and the audience, depending on the situation.

In the hostel, the role of the instrumental superior is played by the staff, whose job it is to exercise social control. The role of expressive superior is taken by the "kitchen regulars," who choreograph the Sunday dinner from beginning to end. The roles of children and extended family are collapsed and assumed by the other visitors, while the marginal role of visitor, switching back and forth between audience and team, is assumed by the volunteers. In that so much depends on the stage manager, we shall examine the duties of the stage manager as they apply to the hostel Sunday dinner, and find surprising parallels.

The kitchen was the locus of all dinner-related activities, and it was here that the kitchen regulars gathered as they arrived. Often several would arrive together, remove their coats, sign up for their regular chores, and rush to the kitchen to prepare a snack. Whatever was in the refrigerator in the form of leftovers was eaten, either cold or warmed up. Tea and coffee were made, places taken at the table, and an excited hum of happiness and anticipation filled the air. Friends who had not seen each other since the previous Sunday related events of the week; those who had, told the rest what they had done together; and the procession into the kitchen was monitored until everyone had arrived. The most frequently asked question of new arrivals was, "Did you get a place?" There was a real sense of "the group," such that if one of the regulars was not there, others began to worry. *Had anyone heard if something had happened to her?* As I became known as one who saw some of the women during the week—for interviews, or to help them find housing—questions were often directed at me if one of my subjects did not turn up. Sometimes I could give information—she had, for example, just moved into a different hostel and was probably tired, or she was ill. The process of keeping tabs on other members of the group signified that the Sunday dinner was ultimately the only regular activity that the women shared, and hence the only sure way of looking out for each others' welfare. There was a strong sense of group loyalty that manifested itself in concern over the welfare of sick, disheartened, or troubled members. The following conversation is a case in point. It occurred when it was clear that one of the group members was not going to come on time, and her friends began speculating about her whereabouts.

> *Regular 1:* She's probably depressed. She's always depressed.
> *Regular 2:* Maybe she's dead.
> *Regular 3:* Oh! How could you say a thing like that!
> *Regular 2:* No, I mean it. She never misses a Sunday, right? What else could have happened to her?
> *Regular 1:* Don't go saying things like that about her.
> *Regular 2:* Well, I say it about all my friends. No sooner do I make friends than they go and die on me. It's the truth. So maybe she's dead.
> *Regular 1:* She's just depressed, that's all. She's always depressed.

My own acceptance into the group as someone who was "okay" came from the shared perception of me as being genuinely concerned with the welfare of the women, and willing to help them outside of the context of the hostel. On one occasion, during the week, I had an appointment to see my physician in the downtown area. In preparation, I dressed "professionally" and boarded a streetcar. To my surprise, one of the regulars was standing at the front of the car, talking with the driver. When she recognized me, she said, loudly to the whole car, "Hey, everyone, this is Lesley, she works at the hostel." We moved to the centre of the car and stood talking until my stop came. She noted my appearance, saying how nice I looked and she didn't know I dressed like that, where was I going, and so on.

I had always known that sooner or later I would encounter one of the women in a different social context from the hostel, and had wondered how I would handle the situation. So, understandably, the next Sunday when I saw her I felt some trepidation. That was quickly dispelled when she approached me almost immediately upon arriving, put her arm around me, and announced to the group, "Lesley's a good kid, on the street she'll talk to you." With my relief came the dawning of a realization that my new-found friends sought simply to be treated with dignity and respect, something that was routinely absent from their lives, and something that the hostel gave them.

1. Planning the Menu and Shopping for Food and Props.
Soon after the greetings and snacking were finished, the kitchen regulars began to plan the dinner menu, with advice and consultation from the staff. They accompanied staff or a volunteer to the food storage area to retrieve goods that were not in the kitchen, and when supplies ran out they were sometimes sent to the store with money to purchase ingredients.

"Insider" and "outsider" statuses were quite rigid. One had to earn the status of inside regular; all others were relegated to the outsider, subordinate status of visitor. I witnessed one woman attempt to break into the clique of regulars. She came into the kitchen and said, "I'm here to help with supper, what are we going to do?" One of the regulars quickly put her in her place: "We're all signed up, we don't need no more supper help." The woman was very stubborn. She planted herself at the table and began to dictate loudly how the quiche should be made. The regulars just ignored her and kept planning the supper with me.

The women generally wanted to have "good" food, and to prepare a good meal with some creative input but not too much work. For many, this was their only opportunity to cook and eat foods that they otherwise could not afford. There evolved a hierarchy of foods, a demand for variety, and, overall, a high level of expectation for the Sunday dinner. The two areas in which these were expressed were in the choice of the main protein course and the dessert course. For the main protein course, it was very important to have meat, and "good" meat at that. The kitchen regulars would complain when the staff told them that the dinner would be macaroni and cheese. This would be considered "cheap" food. If macaroni and cheese were prepared one week, it was assumed that the following week there would be something "really good, because look at all they saved last week when we had that cheap stuff." Popular dishes included turkey, chicken, "bangers and mash," meatloaf, and ham, although pork should be "neither too fat nor too salty."

One week the staff told us that dinner would be beans. One of the regulars was clearly upset.

Regular: Beans! I hate beans! No meat? Tell me something, Lesley, why are we having all these cheap meals? Last week macaroni, this week beans. Why no meat?

Researcher: You're asking the wrong person. I have no idea.

Desserts were special, an opportunity for producing a sweet dish that the women looked forward to all week. Apple pies were always desired, with the kitchen regulars having to make close to twenty pies in order to feed all of the visitors. Two of the regulars dominated the dessert making, giving careful instructions on how to slice the apples ("very, very thin"). Cookies were also very popular, and the "chocolate chocolate chip" cookie became a special treat that the regulars asked for almost every week, but rarely were able to make due to shortages of ingredients. Cookies like these required excessive amounts of "expensive" ingredients like butter, cocoa, and of course chocolate chips, which the hostel does not regularly stock. The approval of the staff to make a special dessert signified that someone would be charged with going to the store and purchasing the needed extra ingredients. This task always fell on someone who could be trusted with the money and with the task of correctly getting the ingredients: the kitchen regulars decided on a delegate to do this, who then got the money from the staff. During the time that elapsed, people would occasionally wonder if the person would take off with the money, only to be reassured by the regulars that "she wouldn't do a thing like that and make us all look bad." This was evidence of the sense of group identity.

One week, the chief dessert maker decided to make chocolate chocolate chip cookies:

Researcher: But you know there aren't any chocolate chips!
Regular: Yeah, but I'm gonna work on [the staff person], maybe she'll give me money to go to the store.

She came back a few minutes later to get her coat.

Regular: I'm going to the store! [huge smile on her face]
Researcher: Oh, you managed that, eh? Do you need cocoa too?
Regular: Oh, yes, we'd better look.

Once when special ingredients were needed, a young woman, who was fondly known as "simple," asked if she could go. The kitchen regulars discussed this among themselves, and decided that it would be good to give her the chance to do something special for the group, although they were worried that she might not bring the right ingredients back. Indeed, when a staff member wrote on a piece of paper what was needed, it became evident that she could not read. The regulars began to speculate about the probability of her coming back as soon as she was out the door:

Regular 1: I hope she gets the right stuff.
Regular 2: Yeah. I'm glad we sent her. She's a sweetie.
Regular 1: Kinda simple, though. You have to tell her everything twice.
Regular 2: I think she'll get the right stuff.
Regular 1: Hope so. Got to give her a chance. If you don't give someone a break they'll never learn, you know.
Regular 2: That's right.

The sense of relief when she later returned, with the proper items and correct change, was palpable.

Another time, macaroni and cheese was to be the main course. The regulars decided that they would make lemon meringue pies for dessert, but in order to do so, eggs and lemon juice were needed. One of their comments indicates the reasoning behind this: "We can send someone to the store. [The hostel] can spring for this since they're not spending any money on the main course".

2. Preparing Food

Preparation for the dinner included the making of the main protein dish, dessert, salads, and a vegetable dish. The division of labour was routine. Two regulars would prepare the protein dish and the dessert, and delegate other duties, such as peeling potatoes. Potatoes were a fairly constant staple dish, with variety coming in the form of having them either served whole or mashed. Often the job of peeling potatoes was assumed by myself. Two other women regularly had the job of preparing the salads. They would remove all of the "salad ingredients" from the refrigerator and begin rinsing, chopping, and adding to the two large stainless steel bowls that would be used to serve it.

The scene in the kitchen in the preparation phase was one of contented business: everyone had their regular post, doing familiar tasks, contributing to the meal. But the routine of preparation served another important function, as a social occasion, reminiscent of "quilting bees" or other collective female activities, where a domestic chore is accomplished within a warm, supportive, sisterly context. The scene in the kitchen was serious, yet carefree: the women were serious about doing a good job, and yet the mood was carefree as it will be when familiar surroundings and friends serve to block out other problems and concerns, if only for a short period of time.

3. Setting the Domestic Stage to Receive Visitors

Throughout the preparation of the dinner, there was a tacit understanding that women who had not signed up to do kitchen duty should stay out of the kitchen. If they did enter, it should only be to get a cup of coffee or tea. The kitchen was, at the time, the exclusive territory of the kitchen regulars, the "back region" where their socializing and cooking was carried out. Whenever an "outsider" intruded, conversation stopped and all eyes were upon the intruder. This was frequently the occasion for boundary maintenance, as the kitchen regulars defined the others as acceptable or not. Their definitions give a clue to the normative structure of the subculture. On one occasion, a visitor came into the kitchen, babbling about being married to Clark Gable and being a spy for the CIA. A regular ordered her out of the kitchen, calling her a "crazy bitch" who was making things up. Afterwards, the group discussed this woman, indicating their rejection of her definition of reality and clearly placing her in a deviant category. Another time, a woman charged in, angrily accusing everyone in sight of having stolen her Bell Calling Card. The kitchen regulars were collectively outraged and virtually tossed her out of the kitchen. The discussions that followed indicated that she was perceived to be "making the whole thing up," including lying about the card's existence in the first place. A third example occurred when one of the regulars had been asked by a staff member if she would be interested in joining a group home that was being set up for some homeless women. Within the subculture, it was generally felt that such an offer would be a golden opportunity to get out of the cycle of homelessness. Yet the woman in question reacted with suspicion, feeling that the staff were lumping her in with other ex-psychiatric patients and defining her as a "basket case." The response from the regulars, who were clearly envious of the offer, is quite telling:

Regular 1:   She's nuts! Most people would be happy to go there! She's being paranoid.

Regular 2:   Yeah, what's the matter with her? She should be grateful. They're giving her a break, getting her off the street for six months.

Regular 3:   She thinks that because it's for ex-mental patients they're going to lock her up; she thinks they think she's a "basket case".

Regular 1:   They're just trying to help her.

One thing that all of the three above examples have in common is the use of terminology referring to mental illness in typifying members as either "normal" or "deviant." It is quite ironic that members defined a woman as "nuts" for being sensitive to institutional definitions of her as being in need of help. This leads one to wonder how institutional definitions of sanity and insanity become internalized by individuals who clearly benefit—in terms of the perpetuation of their dependency—from the continued condition of being "helped" by the institution. Later on, the woman in question approached me on her own to talk about her feelings after having been asked to join the group home.

Regular: I'm worried, I think they want to put me away.

Researcher: But nobody's forcing you to do anything...

Regular: Well, yes they are, in a way...

Researcher: How's that?

Regular: Well, they make me feel trapped.

Researcher: How do they make you feel trapped?

Regular: I'm like a moth, I keep hitting the walls but I can't get out. You know what I mean?

Researcher:	I think I have an idea of what you're saying.
Regular:	They are trying to control me. And I want to be... what I want to be is so far away... I want to be close to my family... I feel like I'm on a see-saw and my side is right on rock bottom. If I get just a drop of kindness it might bring me up even again, you know what I mean?

The kitchen was transformed into a front region whenever a staff person entered. The regulars switched from their close comraderie to assuming a reluctant deference to the authority of the staff person. Usually the regulars were left alone by the staff, especially if a volunteer was in the kitchen keeping an eye on things, but occasionally they would come in and ask for details about how the dinner was going. A regular would usually act as the spokesperson for the group, and any instructions or advice were accepted. Yet, once the staff person left, the kitchen was returned to a back region where disgruntled regulars would complain about the staff member and vent their anger at her interference. "Oh, she goes by the book. Why won't she let us do what we want?" or "Don't listen to her, we'll do it our way and she'll never know the difference" or "She's so tight with money. Who's on next week? Maybe we can make them then."

The other occasion upon which the kitchen became a front region was when dinner was served. In preparation for this, while it was still a back region, several interesting rituals were performed. First, the door to the kitchen was closed. This signified that no one but the kitchen regulars, volunteers, and staff was permitted to enter the kitchen until dinner was served. Second, all personal possessions of the kitchen regulars, like purses and cigarettes—items which were freely left lying around while the kitchen was defined as the back region—were placed in "safe" places, signifying the replacement of trust with mistrust as soon as the visitors were allowed in. Third, plates and cutlery were taken out to the dining room and stacked so that women could get them as they lined up outside the kitchen door. The individual or individuals sent out to perform this task were often mobbed with questions, like "Is it ready yet?," or "What's taking so long in there?" Fourth, the kitchen regulars made up plates for themselves and the staff and volunteers. In reflection of the use of food as a reward, these had the choicest cuts of meat and larger portions than would be dished out to the visitors as they came in. Once a regular sliced off a choice piece of pork and said, "That one's for Lesley." I declined, but was pressured into taking it. These plates were set aside, on the stove, and covered up so that they would not be taken by the visitors. Fifth, the kitchen table was cleared off and set up buffet style. Sixth, the food was laid out on the table. Any decisions on serving size were made at this point, often after a report from the person taking out the dishes on the size of the crowd. If it looked as though they might be short on food, the servers agreed to give smaller servings and save some for seconds. On the other hand, if there was plenty of food and a small turnout, there was a sense of spreading the wealth. Seventh, the regulars were assigned to serve the various dishes and took their positions, ready to serve the dishes that they had prepared; however, if there was going to be a shortage they often asked me to serve. The reason for this was that they did not want to be perceived by the others as cheating them or holding back on food. It was very unpleasant to have to say "no" when the women repeatedly insisted on more food, for it was perceived as a kind of a snub or punishment. Dessert was usually served onto individual plates and set on a counter by the coffee machine, so that the women could take one plate with their coffee. Some took dessert at the same time as their main course, others waited, while some had dessert with no main course. Finally, someone, usually staff or volunteer, called out, "Mums and kids first," signifying that dinner was about to be served, and that women with their children were entitled to the privilege of going first.

4. "Managing" the Performance.

The actual serving of dinner was an interesting performance in itself. As soon as the door to the kitchen was flung open, the kitchen again became a front region, with the visitors filing in to get their food. Most of the time the line was orderly, with the women compliantly waiting. The waiting was usually silent and subdued. As the women approached to get their food, there was never any eye-contact with the server. Instead, they looked down and held out their plates, waited while the food was placed on it, and then moved on to the next server. When they reached the end of the table, they often kept going over to the stove to see if there was any more food, and the regulars had to routinely shout out, "That's it, keep away from there," guarding their own plates.

Management often took the form of handling complaints from the visitors. The kitchen regulars perceived themselves as unappreciated workers who had slaved away all afternoon, and were quite defensive at any complaints that the visitors made about the food. They had to deal with complaints ranging from tastes ("I *hate* green beans," or "Yucch, coleslaw!") to accusations ("Look what you did, you made my spaghetti sauce run into my salad!" or "Why don't you ever make anything good?") to demands ("I need more food, I've been working all day").

Sometimes the routine was broken by an isolated event, such as the time that a severely battered woman appeared in the line. She was emaciated, dressed in minimal clothing, and had bruises over every visible part of her body. She had just received medical care and was wearing a large, white bandage over her right eye, punctuated by a red stain that grew with every moment. Her left eye was swollen and bruised, so that she could barely see out of it. Her mouth was swollen and distorted, and her words were barely intelligible. To the other women, who had all known hard, painful times, she signified their pain, their history, their common condition. All eyes were upon her, welling with tears, emitting compassion. Muffled whispers and gasps conveyed the sorrow that was collectively felt for her. The silent, baleful parade to get food, with eyes lowered, which seemed to isolate and atomize the women, was shattered by the presence of this woman. She had indeed come home, home to a world where no excuses need be made, where no explanation would be required, where she would be accepted. Yet she disrupted the routine precisely because she brought to the surface the reason the rest of the women were there.

Those regulars who were not actively involved in the serving had other important roles, such as monitoring the line. The servers would ask, "How many more to come?" and someone would go out into the hall and report back. The servers would keep serving until the line was gone, and usually this entailed serving up seconds to those who had finished and returned to take a place in line. Then the table was cleared off, with the remaining food being placed on the stove. Any stragglers would serve themselves. Finally, the regulars set the kitchen table for themselves, got out their plates of food, and sat down. At this point, the kitchen was more or less returned to the status of a back region, although there were frequent intrusions from visitors wanting more food, dessert, or coffee.

The regulars always ate at the kitchen table, never in the dining room with the visitors. The staff usually ate in the staff room, either coming into the kitchen to get the plates that the regulars had made up for them, or having them delivered by one of the regulars. I ate in the kitchen with the regulars, something that was noted with appreciation. It was significant that I desired to sit at the table with them rather than in the staff room, and that I was permitted to do so.

While the kitchen regulars ate, they remarked on the different courses and complimented each other on their cooking. Even when dishes had been bungled, which rarely happened, they found something nice to say about the food. This was an important mechanism of affirming, despite the inevitable accusations and complaints from the visitors, that they had done a good job.

5. Cleaning Up the Set

Cleaning up was done by visitors who had signed up for washing dishes. Often resentment was expressed at "having to work," and the staff had to enforce the house rules. For example, one after-dinner exchange went as follows:

Staff:	Did you sign up for dishes?
Visitor:	Yes, I guess so...but I don't want to get dirty.
Staff:	Good, you're needed in the kitchen.
Visitor:	There you go, you have to pay for everything.
Staff:	Yes, we like to put our visitors to work.

For the kitchen regulars, after dinner was a special time for sitting around the kitchen table, quietly smoking and drinking coffee, contemplating the week ahead. As the food was put away, it was not uncommon for the regulars to spirit a chicken leg or a handful of cookies into their pockets or purses; their reward, their secret. *After all everyone's been fed, what harm will it do?* Such actions could never be called stealing.

Conclusion

There are clear parallels between the mythologized ritual of family patriarchy and the play of Sunday dinners within state patriarchy. The breadwinner or instrumental superior role is represented in the roles of the staff and volunteers. As agents of social control, they can exercise sanctions to ensure that the residents, regulars and visitors conform to expected behaviours. The instrumental superior is the source of resources for the meal, including providing access to food storage areas and providing permission and funds to purchase special ingredients. The role of expressive superior is assumed by the kitchen regulars, who occupy a high status in the hierarchy of the clients of the hostel, and serve as stage managers in the performance. From beginning to end, they take responsibility for the dinner, taking control of the kitchen, menu planning, food preparation, performance management, and cleaning up. Visitors are like children in that they are catered to and managed by the regulars, will tend to direct complaints about food and conditions to the regulars, not the staff, and are perceived by the regulars as potentially problematic, untrustworthy, and ultimately unable to look after themselves.

Why are these roles assumed? Why are they played out so closely to the culturally prescribed roles for domesticated women? These issues will be addressed in the next chapter, in which we examine the experience of domesticity within the hostel.

Chapter Seven

"Here I am a Somebody": Residents' Experience of Self

The unidirectional nature of the delivery of most human services means that the recipients rarely are given the opportunity to provide feedback as to how they are experiencing these services. Quite basically, this is because they are cast as dependents on the state who have no other choice but to accept the services as provided, or suffer unaided. I sought to explore the experience of homelessness for the women involved, and to come to an understanding of what the hostel and related services meant to them. I found, despite frequent complaints about living in hostels, that for these women the hostel had taken on a quality of "home." Not only did it provide the necessities of life, but it also provided a network of social support.

Homelessness provides a certain anonymity that few "homeful" individuals can experience or appreciate. Being without a fixed address, without regular employment, without family obligations, and without property—qualities which are by and large interpreted as "deficiencies" within a society in which they have the net result of denying citizenship—also offers a kind of "freedom" from various forms of social control that tie most citizens up in the web of capitalistic and patriarchal relations. For most of the "homeful," a fixed address involves regular payments of rent or mortgage, taxes, and utilities, all of which require a regular income to secure and then to maintain. Thus the private and public realms are mutually interdependent. Family obligations, as noted in Chapter One, are expected and encouraged of citizens, and contribute to the need to maintain a fixed address and regular employment. Social control of citizens is exercised on the basis of such information as identification numbers (address, telephone number, social insurance number, driver's licence, passport, birth certificate, credit cards, bank accounts, medical insurance plans, life insurance plans), and files (taxation records, criminal records, credit records, medical and psychiatric records, education records).

What would it be like to be invisible? To be beyond the arms of state control? To be outside of the control of the domestic unit? To be an anonymous public actor, without any of the ties that bind conventional citizens together? This is the experience of homelessness. Such a condition may be brought about by destitution, but for women it also has its precursors in previous domestic relationships. Women who do not work in the paid labour force and are sequestered to the private sphere of home and family do not, in the beginning, have many of the identification numbers and data files listed above. Most of these are generated in the name of the "breadwinner", who in turn often controls the finances. His name appears on the various insurance policies and plans, and it is his name that ultimately is attached to the fixed address. The connection between the private and the public worlds is precisely through such information. In many ways, then, we may conceptualize the "homeful" woman as already having an anonymity, an invisibility, which is provided by the opaque walls of the domestic unit. It is expected that she will remain inside those walls, doing her domestic duty, precisely because there are few ready-made alternatives. Domesticity is a kind of control in itself, resulting in the self-fulfilling prophecy of women's dependency on men and the family unit. Within the principle of *patria potestas*, women gain their identity only through their role as chattels.

For most of the women encountered, experiences prior to becoming homeless had been characterized by domesticity within the private world rather than autonomy within the public world. On the one hand, this made anonymity almost immediate upon destitution, but on the other hand, it made the prospects of achieving financial independence through paid employment quite grim. The experience of being hurled into the harsh world of publicity, of abject poverty, loneliness, hopelessness, and "disaffiliation" has been the common condition, to varying degrees, of the women who sought emergency shelter. For them, the hostel took on many of the qualities of home.

I was able to speak with many of the informants about their experiences of homelessness and living in hostels. Transcripts of segments of interviews with seven of my informants follow. These were selected in order to suggest the cross-section of backgrounds, ages, and experiences of homelessness among this population.

I. LISA

Lisa was a twenty-one year-old lesbian who had run away from home and come to the city, where she ended up on the street. She had been involved with drug use and drug trafficking, shoplifting, and had spent some time in jail. When we met, she was working at a steady job and was sharing a house with her girlfriend. She still came back to the hostel for

Sunday dinners and felt at home there, both with staff and regulars. Her reflections were those of a woman who had pulled herself up from the mire of homelessness and never wanted to go back.

A lot of people say I'm a good example. I started out traveling here, and then I came here, then I went from hostel to hostel, then I got a job, then I'm out on my own, and I been living where I am for a couple of months, and I like it. I'm stable, I'm fine, and I say look, it's possible. If you want it to work you got to work at it.

Everybody's here for the same reason. Don't know what they're doing or what they're not doing, you know they don't know whether they're coming or going. But people take things from people here in hostels, which I don't like, because everybody's here for the same reason, they have no place to stay, they have family problems or stuff like that, and when people have things ripped off it's not very nice. You know, like a $300 [portable] stereo or a leather jacket.

When I first came here I had no money, no nothing, and a policeman told me about this place and I hopped on the streetcar and I came down, the streetcar driver told me where to get off and I came here, for the first couple of weeks. In order for me to get myself settled I had to go on welfare and find a place, get situated to look for a job. But in the meantime the place where I was living, the sheriff came in and closed the house down because the guy didn't pay the mortgage or whatever. . . and everything was disruptive and stuff, and then the rent went up, in the other places where I lived, and it's just like everything was disastrous from one thing to another, you know? It just didn't quit, just kept going and going and going, and I went from hostel to hostel for awhile, it didn't make any sense, after awhile, I didn't even know what I was doing or where I was going, I was so mixed up.

What did you think of [another hostel]?

It's okay, if you're in a desperate situation and you need a place to stay, anything is okay. Even if you have to sleep on the floor, it's okay, especially if you're really desperate and you want to get your shit together, you know. They're good places to have. But I found there's too many psychiatric patients running around loose in this city. They should do something. They freak me out.

What other kind of people do you run into in hostels?

Hookers, a lot of gay people, people that just have trouble with their parents, young kids who should be in school but they're not. . .

Can you tell me how it feels to be in a "desperate situation"?

You don't know what you're going to do. You just don't. I got really scared, like what the hell am I going to do next, you know? And I didn't know what to do, well I said at least the hostels are here, and if I can get into one that's great, if I can't then I'm really in trouble, I don't even know what I'm going to do, you know?

After I did find a place or whatever, it sort of just went away, but it does, a lot of people after they leave a hostel they don't know where they're going, if they can get into another one, you know?

You do have to have a stable place. You just can't go on from hostel to hostel. You have to have some kind of housing where you can say, look, I can call this home. If I can call this home for as many months or years as I can have this place, I need it. Then they should be able to have it, you know? Because in order for them to get their shit together, to get a job, to go to school, for any amount of reasons, they need it. . . because if you get bumped around all the time you're not going to have nothing, no job, no clothes, no security, no nothing. You have to have some place to live in order to get these things.

Can you tell me how it feels to have a job and a place?

It feels really good. Because if I didn't have a place I don't know what the hell I would do. Probably going from hostel to hostel, living here, living there, doing drugs and this and that. You know, but now I'm situated and I'm stable, and it's great. I wouldn't know what else to do, if I didn't have it. I don't know what I'd be doing now. Out on the street. Instead of what I'm doing every day, is going to work every day, coming home, relax for the evening, watch TV, be a normal person so to speak!

What possessions do you consider to be necessities?

At my place? A bed, food, clothing. TV's and stuff like that aren't really necessities, you don't really need them, but a radio for the news or something, if you want to find out what the weather is, what time it is, if you don't have a clock, yeah, stuff like that, you definitely need stuff like that, if there's no heat in your apartment, a base heater, anything that's important to keep yourself going.

Have you had an apartment with no heat?

I've had apartments with no heat, no water, no showers, no nothin'. I've had dives. And then I've done the work myself, you know, I've fixed it up, I've painted it, and meanwhile the landlord don't give you a break, and when you move out he just raises the rent for somebody else, and it's all fixed up.

What does the word "home" mean to you?

In a home environment, everything should be going smoothly, I don't like people that fight a lot and stuff like that. When you're fighting all the time the atmosphere is disruptive. All the agony, aches and pains, stuff like that. *A good environment, a good loving environment, a good relationship, that's great. It doesn't matter the possessions, it's what people are there.*

II. CLAUDIA

Claudia was a thirty-one year old East Indian woman whom I met at the hostel and saw regularly at the drop-in centre as well. She was an ex-psychiatric patient who had been released five years before, and was on family benefits. She lived in an adjoining room to her boyfriend's, who was in a similar situation. She spoke of how she managed with her meagre funds, and her hopes for the future.

I don't go for looks or money. What's important to me is trust: forgive and share. We have been living together for two years. I want to get married and have a child.

Where we live, our landlord is very strict. We share a kitchen, and we can't even get up in the middle of the night to make tea. It's not very comfortable cooking there. We can't eat in the kitchen, we have to eat in our rooms. The landlord is crazy sometimes, he makes a lot of noise in the morning just to make a cup of tea. If we did that, we'd be out of there!

Our rent just went up $10 a month each, but our cheques went up $15, so we have $5 left over each. That makes a big difference. I budget myself $7 a day for everything: food, coffee, cigarettes. I won't go over it. I can get jeans for $8 and a purse for $12 at this discount store.

Our rooms are furnished. I have my own bedding, my sister gave me a blanket. My boyfriend's bed is bad, you can feel the springs. The landlord might give him a new one. I have a good bed.

I would love to have a job. I have been working at the rehab place for almost four years. If I work for a whole week I get $22. They give you light factory work, counting bolts and putting them in a package. If you work hard enough and long enough they try to get you a real job. I don't go in every day, I've given up on ever getting a real job because I've been there so long and they haven't given me one. I'm too old—they want young people who will work for them for a long time. I get my medication there, shots and pills.

When I first came to Canada I used to work in accounts receivable at a company. I still remember my job. Then I got sick. I used to be very violent and angry, they call it schizophrenic. I've been on medication for five years, it has helped a lot. But I tell my doctor that medication isn't everything. It's only about thirty percent of what you need to get well.

What else do you need?

God. I pray every morning and every night that I won't get sick again.

Did you lose touch with God when you were sick?

Yes [sadly], I lost my religion for a long time.

How do you like coming to the drop-in centre?

It's good to have a place to go during the day. I like to sit and talk, it helps to pass the time. I could stay at home with my boyfriend, but he's always there. I need to get out. I go to the hostel on the weekend. It's nice to go there and see friends and do some chores. On Saturdays I always go and visit my sister.

You can save a lot of money by having lunch and coffee at the drop-in centre, and Sunday dinner at the hostel.

Yes, but I would pay. I don't come here to save money, I come to have the company. I would pay five dollars a week—if they asked for it—just to come here. And the hostel, well there I save money, that meal is worth five dollars you know. I don't eat breakfast and lunch, and I save money.

III. ADRIAN

Adrian was a thirty-five year-old black woman with two children, nine and eight years old. She left her husband when she could no longer tolerate his violent abuse, and they had now been separated for three years. Despite the fact that he had "a good job," he had not provided any support for herself or her children. She had been evicted from her apartment and was staying at a hostel while trying to find another place. A single mother, she was attempting to gain her grade twelve certificate. She had been laid off from her job several months before, and was currently on welfare.

Well, a house isn't all there is to life. A house is nice to furnish and everything, but if there's no communication and you are a second-class citizen in your spouse's eyes—what's the point?

What does home mean to you?

It's not financial security, because I had that. I guess when two people are really compatible. . . like. . . we kind of share everything—that communication—you don't feel like you're being left out. A place where you're not treated like a housekeeper.

Can you describe how it feels to not know where you're going to be living?

I don't know if there are any words, especially when you have children. It's a feeling like you don't belong anywhere, you know?

What will make you feel like you belong?

What I need more than anything is a place to live—it doesn't have to be big, I can't afford a big place—something clean, something liveable so you can get along with your life.

Is it important to you to have your own private space?

Yes, it's extremely important, I should say.

What is it about having your own place that makes you feel like you belong?

I feel very contented when I'm in my own place with my children, doing the things that I like to do, and not because I have to do them for someone else or to please someone else. You know, like I don't have to make the beds because if I don't someone will come home and hit the roof.

What things do you like to do? Do you have any hobbies?

Cooking, reading, I love to entertain if I can afford it—to have people over to talk, play cards. . .

It must be hard for you to do that now.

Yes, I haven't done that for quite awhile. If I had money I'd love to travel, take my kids everywhere, see the world. I like to mix with people, to talk, to get to know people. I'm not the kind of person that's fine alone.

What do you imagine when you think about the difference between having a place and not having a place?

I'll feel like an adult again—I feel like a little child that runs away from home—you know? You don't have a special place, you're here today, there tomorrow. I'll feel like an adult again—make my own decisions about simple things you take for granted. . .

Like what?

I have nothing against those places [hostels]—they are there to help people like me—but you feel like a child again, like your rights are taken away. There are rules, like you have to come in at a certain time—I guess they're needed.

IV. APRIL

April was a forty year-old woman who had been on the hostel circuit for several years. After a nervous breakdown, she had been in a psychiatric care centre for "a long, long time," then, as she says, "they put me on tranquilizers and I couldn't even think for years." She had never been married nor had children, and had lost the few jobs that she had attempted. Due to her psychiatric history she had been defined as permanently unable to work, and received a monthly family benefits cheque. She spoke of the "rut" of homelessness and how hard it was to get out of it.

I know even if you have all of your senses together it's still hard to find a job and to find a place to live that's decent and that. People that are quite capable and qualified to find jobs and still don't. If you have a job, you know, a fairly decent job, then it's a lot easier to find a place. It's the only way that I can think to, you know, get out of this rut!. . . hostels and rooms and stuff like that. . . yeah. . .

This one place I lived. . . it was awful, people playing their stereo all night. I ended up staying on the subway all night and sleeping during the day.

You rode the subway all night?

Yes, I've done that several times. At least, until the guards tell me to get off, and then I have stayed out for twenty-four hours wandering the streets. I've met some very weird people on the streets at night, some weird men, I've had some terrible experiences. And that night the cops stopped me twice. But when I was on the subway they asked me where I was from and I said I had a terrible room and couldn't sleep and just rode around to have a safe place to sit and they said I would have to get off. They wanted to know what was wrong, why I sat there just staring into space, and I said that I'd had a nervous breakdown and that I spent some time in the [psychiatric hospital]. . . . But they still told me I had to get off, that the subway is not to be used for that kind of thing, that you have to have a purpose for riding it.

Can you describe to me what your feelings are about living in a hostel?

It's driving me crazy. I can hardly wait to get out. I didn't want to go. They were driving me crazy so much I stayed in a laundromat for a few days!

What does the word "home" mean to you?

I'm having trouble relating right now. I think, I know some people say that home is where you hang your hat. But a lot of times I didn't even have a hat! I don't know. For a lot of other people. . . it's hard for me. When I was living in a lot of places I tried to imagine what I'd like a home to be and try to wish they were that way. But a lot of them weren't. And I wasn't happy in a lot of them. But they were nice places, they were okay. . . If you're living by yourself it may be different. But I think if you're living with other people a home has to be a place where you feel, where you feel comfortable, where you feel happy and where you feel, maybe just where you can relate, you can grow and do what you need and be what you need and what you want and just, you know, where you can live, really.

What do you do after Sunday dinner at the hostel?

Well, sometimes we go out for a walk. We sit around and tell each other crazy stories, but unfortunately usually they're true. . . they usually happened to someone.

Does time go by quickly in the evening?

[Sarcastically] Oh yes, we're so busy it just flies by. Yeah, we have so much to do we never know where the time goes.

I had helped her to make contact with a place out of town where she would be staying. She was very excited and had to catch a bus in the afternoon. I offered to drive her to the bus station, and on the way to help her to pick up her things.

> I got to get my stuff. I left one big bag and one little bag at [a local discount store where she had bought a few things to take with her], and I said, keep it for me . . . until tomorrow, until today, and I've got some stuff in a locker, *two* different lockers downtown—one at the, um [subway station] locker and one right at the bus station, subway locker.

> *Do you have bags, a suitcase or anything?*

> No, no, I think I should have ended up with a garbage bag or something, but I might end up getting a back pack but I don't think I can get all my stuff in it.

> *Could you tell me why you are taking the possessions that you are taking with you?*

> I don't even know why. I looked at them and thought, you know, why am I even carrying this stupid stuff. . . Why should I bother carrying it all the way out there?. . . I don't like, when I go out for a walk, the way I really like to walk, like I just like to walk, eh? I hate purses, I don't even buy them, I threw away all the purses I had, I threw away all my watches cause I don't like keeping track of time. . . I just got rid of all my jewellery and I'm glad I threw it away, I really am. . . and you know, all this clutter and paraphernalia, you know you feel so great when you get rid of it.

V. ROSEMARY

Rosemary was a fifty-four year-old woman who was on long-term disability insurance after having done heavy paid domestic work for many years. She had been in and out of hostels, rooming houses, and marginal housing. When I met her, she was in an unhappy situation with an abusive landlord, and was looking for a "better place"

> I was married for two years. One year of my marriage was very happy, and I thought that would last for a lifetime. But in the second year my husband found another girl, and after that he treated me very bad. I did take this for a year, but after that I couldn't take it. One morning I woke up and couldn't take it, I ran away. He beat me up. A few times. He's the one who was wrong and he beat me up so badly. I couldn't take it no more.

> *And you never got married again or had another serious relationship with a man?*

> No. I know a ... man, and I knew him for quite a while, but one day he kicked me, and we was very close to getting engaged, you know, I liked him a great deal ... I said to myself, he's just like my husband. And I just left him. And after that I never, I never even look at a man. I was so hurt, I said not again. I can't.

If you had the opportunity to live the way you would like to live, what would you want?

I only would like to have my own little apartment. . . no matter how small it is. Because I'm so shy, I only feel comfortable, okay I lock my door and I'm private, you know? And maybe someday I will have my own place.

What does working mean to you?

Well, that would make my life fulfilled, you know? And if I would be able to support myself, I would feel much better about myself, but while I'm not working I feel so useless, so. . . . I don't like the government to support me because at least I should be able to work another ten years, and I would feel more respectable, you know? *Sometimes I feel like I'm in the middle of nowhere. I'm too old to be retrained, and too young for the senior citizen benefits.* . . . And you see, sometimes when I work here a lot [at the hostel, doing chores], I like to bury myself, you know? Like to be busy, like you sort of don't think of your problems, which is very good for me.

Why do you think it is that you feel good at [the hostel]?

Well, first of all I feel like all the girls I meet there, you know, there's some kind of a trouble. Whoever checks in or visits, I know we are all equal. . . . I feel good about it because I know there is nobody who looks down at you. . . and the staff is so good to you, you and all the staff, they make you so welcome there. When I look at this one or the other, I say you know they all just suffering and then I don't bear it all alone, you know? And especially when I live there for two weeks. I feel so secure. Nobody here can attack me, I was treated by men so bad, I sort of feel so secure, and it's very nice if you know out there is somebody when you are in need or in trouble to help you. . . . And I look forward to every Sunday, to see my friends. Like when I lived in rooming houses, like mostly they treat you like dirt because you are poor or you're unable to work and you have to live with it. My landlady many times said I'm just like trash, and I don't think she's any better than me. You know, just because they own a home and the next guy doesn't. We had a beautiful home too, you know, if my husband would be half a decent man I still would have a home. And we was not poor, we belonged to the middle class, you know, we were not rich rich, but we was not poor too. We was quite well off, you know? We all worked in our family, nothing but work, work, but we had the money too. And that gave me self-respect. But just here, because I don't have a home, people treat you like you are a nobody.

You said that you hate to feel like everything you have is in plastic bags. . .

While I was home I had a nice closet and my dresses was hanging neatly in my closet and I didn't need any shopping bags, I didn't wander around from one place to the other, because where I lived I said that's my home, and that's where I stay. There are days when I think, why do I have to move so often? Why am I always at the end of my line? Why is that? Why can't

I find the right place and I don't have to move anymore? You know, when you move in a new place you have to adjust to so many things. First, when you move in it's always a different location. Then you have to get used to the home, the atmosphere, and I don't know, to me it takes quite a while until I really feel at home, you know like comfortable, to say okay that's my home.

What is home to you?

[The hostel].

That's right, isn't it?

Well, thank God I have now two weeks I can relax, you know? Well, this is home to me because I feel so comfortable. At [the hostel] I can do, like in the daytime, okay, we go out and look for a room and do one thing at a time, but I can do what I really [want], I go home and do my little chore and [if] I feel like [it] I watch television, the staff are very nice to me, and you are very nice to me, everybody is good to me, it's home, you know?

So before, you had a middle-class life, you had everything you needed, and a nice house, but it wasn't home?

It was no home because there was no happiness. I know I was not wanted, you know?

What do you do during the day?

Usually in the morning I go to the shopping centre. By the time I get there I'm *hungry*, you know, that's the first thing I start my day. It's usually about eleven, twelve, you know, then I have a good meal, and then I go window shopping. I know it's funny but it's something to do with my time, you know? Especially I love to look at the materials, I say, maybe one of these days I'm gonna make a dress. . . . And then I go to the library, and I sort of look at the magazines, but I'm not a great reader. Or I look at the newspaper, you know, and then I go back to the mall again and have a little bite. And sometimes I run into a girl I know, I used to know, and we talk a little. . . . I don't go to church, but I pray every day. I don't go to church, I look so shabby. In the church people are dressed up, they have a hair-do and all that, I cannot go. But I believe in God.

I'm sure you can find a church where you can go and feel comfortable.

Oh, I do go to [a Church], I drop in during the daytime when it's empty, I just go and pray there, and this is just as good as, you know. I do go.

Does the day go quickly for you, when you go out?

Yeah, I find that my time goes by, but when I sit home, sometimes to me when I look at the alarm clock it looks like the time goes backwards.

How do you forget about your problems?

Keep yourself busy, occupied. If you sit idle you just think about your problems.

When Rosemary left her boarding situation and went to the hostel, she left most of her things behind.

Have you decided whether you should go back and get your things or not?

I think I'll leave it there because the taxi these days is so expensive, on the money I can, well, I don't know if it's worth it, you know?

What do you own? What would you be leaving behind?

What I mostly would treasure is my alarm clock. At least you want to know your time. And then I have a TV, then I have a radio.

You have all these things and you'd be willing to leave them behind?

Yeah, because I cannot afford. And then I have a few clothes, I mean they are good, they are good enough to wear, but of course clothes, even if [the hostel] gives me one more suit, that's enough for me. But at least the time, I would like to know. Because if I move I don't know if I can afford an alarm clock, you know? But on the other hand, I'm not sure if I can afford the taxi, so. . .

Can you tell me where you get most of your clothes from?

Everything I own is from [the hostel].

And you don't have boots, do you?

I have no boots, but I did save up for the boots, but my worker looked up in my bank book and she said, I have too much money, but I saved it up for the boots . . . and they take off that money.

From your [monthly disability] cheque?

Yes. . . . But they should encourage people to save. I should have my right to do with my own money whatever I please. You see, since I have so little money on welfare, this is actually where I really learned how to save. . . . But I saved so hard, every penny when I spend it I look twice or three times just to make sure. And I denied myself from so many things and they take it away from me. You know, this is also injustice. You know? I didn't even do any laundry. I didn't buy myself as much as a nylon, or any, not even a package of kleenex, this is really denying. And yet when it is taken away from you, your own money, you know that hurts.

What do you deny yourself?

Well, for example, I was just dying for a purse for so long. I was so ashamed with that shabby purse. But I said, if I buy a purse then I have to buy shoes too. I wouldn't feel comfortable to have a nice purse and shabby shoes. But then I said, maybe then I cannot pay my rent. I'll just have to wait till I find something in the donations room. I call this denying myself because, even nylons, you know, for example yesterday I found a new pair of nylons in the hostel and to me this is a luxury because I don't want to spend money on nylons. And every little thing. . . it costs maybe today, well I don't even look at the price, maybe about two dollars. You see that's two dollars I can save. *And since I couldn't take a bath I didn't even buy soap. I had a little bit of soap that was given to me for Christmas, and this is all very useful to me, or sometimes I win in bingo a nice little bar of soap, and of course if I can take a bath I save on the soap too.*

At the housing office, I located a possible room for Rosemary. She returned from looking at it and told me what had happened. The landlord had asked her if she had a TV, a radio, or anything, and she had said, "No, I don't have anything," because she had left her things at her previous place. To this the landlord replied, "I don't want any trash in this place."

VI. TAMARA

Tamara was a fifty-eight year-old woman whom I saw frequently in the hostel and at the drop-in centre. She had been married for thirty years, and had been homeless for the past six. Her lifestyle involved living in hostels during the winter and living outside during the summer. she did not have a steady source of income, and vehemently refused to apply for welfare, claiming that she was "free" the way she was and she liked it. Due to her life of "permanent transiency" she had very few possessions: one was a large bag in which she carried pop bottles which she collected and cashed in; another was a sleeping bag in which she slept by the side of the road in the warm summer months. Tamara was very eloquent and somewhat philosophical in her descriptions of her life:

I'm in the best part of my life: no more periods, no worry about getting pregnant—I have the future to look forward to. I abstain from sex. Face it, what else do you need a man for besides sex and companionship? I don't have sex any more and I can get companionship just as well from a woman. I don't need a man to take care of me. I can do everything a man can do. I am an electrician, I can do plumbing, I can fix machines, I can fix just about anything. At our house someone had stolen the beautiful brass doorknobs from our bathroom and I kept pestering my husband to get new ones. Finally after a few months he came home from Canadian Tire with new ones. I thought he would put them on himself, but he handed them to me. I didn't need to look at the instructions, but I locked myself in the bathroom! I had to take the whole lock off in order to get out!

We had a nice house on a big piece of land. I had three kids—two boys and a girl—all champions! My eldest son went in for military training instead of finishing high school, and he came out at the top of his class in marksmanship and got a little plaque. My next son was a goalie and on the all-star team of the community.

How do you feel about staying in hostels?

I don't like it much, people are pretty sloppy, crap on the toilet seat, leave garbage lying around. Why do they do that? Women should have nice feminine rooms—pastel colours, nice matching bedspreads and drapes. I wish the hostels were nice like that. When I dream of a bedroom, I think of white...crisp, frills, eyelet. I left my bedroom suite and all of my belongings in the house.

Do you know what happened to your things?

No, maybe one day I'll find them at the Salvation Army and buy them back.

How do you feel about sleeping outside?

I love it! In the summer I walked to [a city about fifty miles away] three times. It took a long time, but when I got tired I just found a soft place by the side of the road to sleep on. No one ever bothers me, not even the mosquitoes.

I get a cold once a year but I know how to handle it. I don't like spending a lot of time indoors because that's unhealthy. I like fresh air. My philosophy of dressing: layers, lots of *thin* layers, keeps you warmer than just one heavy sweater.

Once, I was sleeping on the ramp at City Hall, by the hot air vent. I would make a little shelter for myself out of cardboard boxes. That kept the cold wind off me, and then the warm air coming from the vent made a very cozy place to sleep.

Do you go there often?

Just to sleep. One night I was just dozing off when I got kicked in the head! This guy put the boots to me! I was already vulnerable, lying on my back, but then when I was half asleep getting kicked in the head I was not capable of fighting back. He kicked me brutally a few more times, ripped off my pants and raped me. After he left, I dragged myself all the way over to "emerg" at the hospital. *When I got there, beaten and raped, the doctor asked me if he should call the police! I said, what do you think? Look at me! Of course you should call the police!*

I don't care much for the police. I get in fights with them a lot. They tell me to "move along" and I tell them I have a right to be there just like anyone else. One time in the subway station I was carrying two shopping bags full of clothes. I hadn't had a chance to wash them in awhile, so they were a little dirty, but they were my clothes! A policeman, or it might have been a company cop, grabbed my bags and put them in the garbage. I put up a fight and told him to give them back to me. We ended up wrestling on the platform! He was huge! And he tried to push me onto the tracks! Finally he let his hands fall to his sides and I again demanded that he give me back my things. He went over to the garbage can and took them out.

You know, now that I've lived this way I don't think I could ever be settled again. What if I had a nice house—I'd have the four walls and then I'd be bored. This way I am always learning, always meeting new people, every day is different. But I never thought in a million years I'd end up this way.

VII. EVELYN

Evelyn was a sixty year-old woman who had been married and had one daughter, with whom she did not get along. I met her at the housing office, where she often dropped in to chat with the workers. A bitter woman, she told me that she had been a "damn good secretary," she had even been an executive secretary, but that through a series of tragic events she had descended on the downward spiral to the "skids," and had never been able to pull herself up. Her idea of home was clearly tempered by years of poverty and living in marginal housing.

I feel homeless, I feel as though I'm living in the waiting room of a railway station. It's like you're in between. Where you've come from is not that important any more but you're not sure where you're going. . . . I'm not enamoured of this city because of course I've been living on the underbelly of it. A large city is merciless to those who have no money. .

What home do you foresee for the future, for you to look forward to?

A reasonably decent, self-contained apartment. And *privacy*—with *my* things.

The "mine" seems very important to you.

The "mine" is everything. I want my books, my music to surround me. No one could come in without being invited first. Even if it wasn't much it would be good. I could be alone as I want. . . . I suppose my biggest problem is that I have a champagne taste on a beer budget. . . . I can't tell you too much about home because all I've ever had is me and that's all I know. But I do know that it's not in a rooming house.

Do you have any possessions?

Yes, I used to have furniture, but I lost it because . . . I. . . couldn't afford. . . the storage [breaks down]. . . . I lost my possessions, my cat, and my daughter. . . . But it's nothing that a regular salary can't mend [stiff upper-lip]. If only I had money. . . just to get started again. . . . It's awful being on welfare—what a terrible feeling. I could get more money—I'm sixty and I'm now eligible for family benefits. But that means I have to be registered as "permanently unemployable." I don't want that. I want to work. But I have very high blood pressure, the doctor says I may have a stroke. I suppose that is reason enough to be unemployable.... I could supplement it with a part-time job, that's what I'd like. But with family benefits you're not supposed to work.

What do you do during the day?

Mostly, I stay in my room. There's no one to talk to that shares my interest, and I hate gossip, small talk. I try to listen to my radio, it's all I have, I try to read but it's so hard with the music [loud music coming from the other roomers in the building].... I tried putting cotton in my ears...

Being dependent on the public, having to go to a hostel—I went to [the hostel] and then to [another hostel]—it was sheer hell. Now that I know. . . if only I'd known then. When I first went there, I had my nose in the air. I didn't realize how much I was on the skids.

[The hostel] was sheer hell?

[The hostel] has been great, I can't find enough words for how much they try.... But I felt at the bottom of the world, at the bottom of a well. *I'm too young for a pension, too old to be hired seriously. It's a hell of a limbo.* As far as housing goes, you're at a disadvantage to start with because you don't know what you're getting into. Now I know. Someone should write a book about women who are between forty-five and sixty-five years old, now that's a sad story. Something should be done about it.

As the above excerpts suggest, the experience of homelessness has a devastating, debilitating effect on women's sense of their selves. Time stops; one's life ceases to develop further, to progress. One can no longer look to the future with hope, only to the past with nostalgia and regret. The days become endless, meaningless struggles to "put in time," and in the public sphere one is constantly reminded of the devalued status of the homeless in a society in which homefulness is valorized. Needs become redefined ("going without" many items that most people take for granted in order to save up for a pair of boots, for example), and one is chronically, painfully aware of one's poverty and exclusion from the mainstream economy of production, consumption, and reproduction. The necessity of "travelling light" means that one's possessions are pared down to absolute minima: an alarm clock, a few clothes, the omnipresent cigarettes. Perhaps most crippling is the painful aloneness. For women who were for the most part socialized to see their lives fulfilled when seeing to the needs of others, this is particularly dispiriting.

The spectre of the women sitting at the table, smoking cigarettes and drinking coffee, holding their heads in their hands, putting in time, assaulted my senses that first day at the hostel. Through the hours of conversations, interviews, and observation, I traveled the long road of learning why, learning that homelessness is a deep hole, an abyss from which for many there is no exit. One event crystallized this collective experience. At the drop-in centre, there were about ten women sitting around a large table, quietly engaged in various activities. Two women were playing Scrabble, several were knitting, a few were staring into space. Without warning, a young woman began to cry softly. As the tears flowed down her face, two of the others went over to comfort her. The rest stopped what they were doing and began to cry as well. Not a word was spoken, but entire worlds were shared.

In that grey, shadowy world of homelessness, disengaged from the arrangements of time and space which hold together the rest of the society, the hostel becomes much more than an emergency shelter. It sheds a kind of light and warmth that lonely souls crave. Through the hostel, the women were able to overcome anonymity and reestablish a semblance of "homefulness." How is it possible for a hostel to become a home?

As was suggested in Chapter One, the mythologized "home" serves as the realm of expressivity: comfort, security, enduring family relations, mutual acceptance. It also serves as the context for biological and social reproduction, and the playing out for women of the roles of wifework, housework, and motherwork (Rosenberg, 1986). It is contrasted with the public realm, which is the realm of instrumentality: paid employment, "the market." The public realm provides the resources for the establishment of the private realm, enabling breadwinners to economically support, through the family wage, the costs of purchasing and maintaining a house, and supplying the consumption needs of family members.

"Homeless women" have as their common condition the lack of a private realm, and come to the hostel in search of the physical provision of shelter. But for those who stay, who become the "chronically homeless" or the regulars, the hostel takes on many of the expressive features normally associated with home. The women are able to make and take the roles normally associated with expressive superiors, with the major exception being the set of roles associated with wifework (for example, having sexual relations with the patriarch, seeing to his needs, etc.).

The hostel is experienced as a home both physically and socially. The regulars fiercely defend their hostel, as one would defend one's home. Complain as they might about rules and limited resources, they are committed to preserving what they have. The continuing availability of the hostel for Sunday dinners, which provides the only regular meeting time and place in their community, might be threatened in several ways. It might be threatened physically, by fire for example. There were two occasions on which the threat of fire evoked strong reactions in the regulars. On one occasion, there was some smoke emanating from the hostel's garbage outside. Within a few seconds of detection, the fire alarm had been set off, the hostel was emptied, and one of the regulars had grabbed a fire extinguisher and run out to douse the fire. As the women circled the smouldering garbage, there was a palpable sense of mutual fear, fear of the potential loss. The threat of fire had brought them together to defend their home. On another occasion, a woman was making popcorn on the stove. She neglected the pot for a few minutes, and the oil began to smoke. One of the regulars jumped up from the table, removed the pot from the heat, and angrily turned to the woman, saying "What are you trying to do? Burn the place down? If you do that we won't have a Christmas dinner!"

Another possible threat to the home was the violation of house rules. Regulars were circumspect on all occasions, ensuring that they did not do anything to aggravate staff. The cost of being barred was tantamount to being thrown out by one's family. And whenever any visitor exhibited behaviour that could threaten the home—such as swearing, fighting, or "acting crazy"—the regulars were quick to defuse the situation and warn the perpetrators of the implications for all. While on the one hand, members of the community felt themselves a close-knit group, with internal norms of reciprocity in which the staff were often framed as "the enemy," there was also a shared sense of what was appropriate and inappropriate behaviour, based on the collective interests of the group. This was evident in the following after-dinner exchange:

> *Researcher:* Oh yeah, I heard that _____ got barred for three months, eh?
> *Regular 1:* Yeah, and she's mad at us because she thinks we snitched on her. We didn't. The staff asked me and I didn't want to snitch so I said she was "high on life."
> *Regular 2:* The staff aren't blind, you know. They noticed eventually. Remember a few years back that woman got barred. . .
> *Regular 1:* Yeah, for putting something in the food. Now that's a good reason. I would tell the staff if someone was going to hurt other people.

The women for whom the hostel had become a home, then, closely monitored both physical and social threats to their home, and were quick to provide sanctions.

The sense of fair play also extended to treatment of "their own." Anyone who suffered undue hardship (among women who were all living through difficult times) was treated with extra sympathy. When one regular was in hospital, her friends visited her several times during the week, and brought back progress reports on Sundays. Special selections of dessert or bingo prizes were reserved to take to her in the hospital, with the implicit approval of all of the regulars.

Staff were ranked according to how they treated the regulars. Those who went out of their way to accommodate the women, such as helping them move in their off-hours, or bending the rules in the hostel, were highly regarded, while those who were perceived to feel hostility or mistrust of the women were met with hostility and mistrust in return.

Once I was walking downtown with one of my informants, who was also a Sunday regular, on our way to check out a room that we had found out about at the Housing Office. We ran into another Sunday regular:

Regular 1:	Look who's there!
Regular 2:	Look who we got here! It's Lesley!
Regular 1:	Hi!
Regular 2:	Hi! So what are you doing? Are you going to find her a place?
Researcher:	Yeah.
Regular 2:	Good girl. Well, I'll be seeing you Sunday.

When it was made common knowledge that I had helped one regular find a new place, I was positively sanctioned with remarks like, "Thank you for treating her so well. She deserves it, you know," while her abusive ex-landlord was framed as "evil" and "mean.

Another interesting expression of the responsibility that the regulars felt for the hostel came when we ran out of bingo prizes and had to stop playing. Two regulars appeared the next week with bags of small prizes that they had personally purchased. The prizes consisted of inexpensive samples of shampoo and hand cream, falling into the category of "most desirable" prizes. They were received with much gratitude by the others, who recognized the gesture as a kind of personal sacrifice that was very highly valued.

The women making up the subculture of homelessness experienced the hostel as a home both physically and socially. They gravitated toward a safe shelter where subsistence needs could be met by access to food, tokens, bingo prizes, tobacco, and clothing. But equally important was the community of like-others, where women who felt themselves to be systematically devalued in public were able to reproduce the close-knit, trusting warmth of home. At the hostel they could count on friendship, understanding, and mutual respect. They could live out roles they had been prepared for, and be rewarded for excelling as expressive superiors. They could reproduce a modicum of control in the kitchen and in the management of Sunday dinners. They could cook, shop, eat, and dress in away that was otherwise far beyond their means. And they could forget, albeit temporarily, the cold world of "publicity" in which they were defined as homeless. For here, among their "family," they had a home.

Chapter Eight

When a Hostel Becomes a Home:
The Cycle of Dependency

When a hostel becomes a home, there is an intersection between women's experiences of home and the stated aim of social services to provide them with one. Despite the positive experience of home felt in the hostel by the women studied, the implications of the reproduction of domesticity must be examined. The latent functions of the social services for homeless women include the perpetuation of dependency, the reinforcement of expressive roles, and the displacement of status such that women become powerless in relation to the more powerful staff, and ultimately in relation to the state. At the hostel, women "pay their keep" by doing familiar household chores. At the drop-in centre, they are expected to find personal fulfillment and gratification in improving their appearance, accumulating clothes, and performing mundane tasks such as knitting and watching soap operas that are generally associated with "just a housewife" roles.

This confluence often results in a downward spiral of dependency, which takes the form of chronic homelessness. Access to housing services, a free telephone, and newspaper listings are often unused. One respondent sat for days outside of the housing office, complaining that she was in an "emergency housing situation," yet refusing to venture inside, where housing might be found for her. She was later encountered in both the hostel and the drop-in centre aimlessly flipping through pages of the newspaper, conveniently skipping the "Rooms For Rent" ads and instead reading such articles as "Dear Abby." She admitted to having been in this state for at least two years.

The hostel and day-time drop-in centre contribute to the displacement of female dependency from the family to social services. Female expressive roles are reinforced with emphasis on powerlessness, lack of autonomy, replication of domesticity, and idolation of feminine beauty. Together, these constitute a comfortable alternative to the horrors of the past—an ironically protective "haven in a heartless world" (Lasch, 1977).

Powerlessness. The staff-resident relationship is one in which the resident must conform to the wishes of the staff person and the rules of the house in order to be granted permission to stay at the hostel. The staff, out of organizational necessity, take on "instrumental superior" roles and reproduce patriarchal relations by creating a situation in which women have no choice but to be dependent upon them. Staff, in turn, feel powerless to engage in more than a "band-aid" approach. Most, as committed feminists, find it particularly discouraging that their position forces them to be part of a larger structure with which they do not always agree, and to adopt a "policing" rather than a "helping" role much of the time. Above all, they feel discouraged in the face of the desperate shortage of housing, which they consider to be the major cause of the problem and the most important place to begin to ameliorate it.

Lack of autonomy. Lack of autonomy occurs when women are thrown together with strangers in the most intimate of living arrangements. Lack of privacy coupled with the constant fear of victimization by other residents contributes to a generalized feeling of objectification among residents. It is difficult to develop a sense of efficacy—a prime component of instrumentality—when confinement so resembles what Garfinkel (1956) termed "degradation ceremonies."

Replication of domesticity. The structuring of household chores in the hostel and day-time activities in the drop-in centre serve to replicate a domestic world typical of that for which successfully socialized "expressive" females are equipped. Yet days go by with few or no structured opportunities to break out of that model. The structure creates a self-fulfilling prophecy in which domesticity becomes "all there is to do."

Idolation of female beauty. Perhaps the most telling indication of the lingering relevance of expressivity is the emphasis placed on appearance, particularly at the drop-in centre. Whether it is the result of the well-intentioned staff, or whether it is the undying desire for visual approval by peers, this emphasis (in the form of free wardrobe, makeup, manicure and hair dressing) becomes an end in itself. This reinforces the dimension of expressivity which idolizes feminine beauty and relies on peer approval of appearance for a positive self-image.

The tragic unintended consequence of the reproduction of domesticity for those who become chronically homeless is that it deadens the spirit, it weakens the will, and it makes it all too easy to subsist in idle, timeless dependency. It is possible to go literally from one hostel to the next for years on end, with no source of income. Food, shelter, clothing, and transportation are all provided. The hostel circuit comes to replace home, to be the only alternative to a "conventional" home. Many women frame the experience as a kind of punishment for their own failure, as the following excerpt from an interview reveals:

Well, I think about once I had it so good, you know? And why do I have to live in plastic bags, and you know what I think I should have a home...

Well, all I do in my life is move. And I'm always scared because it's difficult to live in other peoples' homes, it's, if you know you have your own home you feel comfortable, you know? I try so hard to not think about those things, but that lives with you, you know? I wonder if everybody feels like that if they have to move so often, if they take it so hard too, I don't know.

The downward spiral of the hostel system is a familiar fact to social workers who have become involved with the plight of homeless women. The vocabulary of the hostel workers, an important cultural indicator, attests to this (Spradley, 1980). The "hostel circuit," or more familiarly, the "circuit," is the constellation of hostels that are frequented by the "regulars." "Regulars" are women who have basically given up any hope of getting out of the circuit. They often weave elaborate dreams of finding "a place," but when the opportunity presents itself, for example when a well-intentioned worker comes upon "a place," invariably it "doesn't work out." "Doesn't work out" to a regular seems to boil down to a problem with her own sense of herself, as much as with the place. It is too hard to handle having one's own place: the loneliness, the fear, the squalor of the rooming houses. But overwhelmingly, there is one reason for "not working out" which resounds: it means taking responsibility for one's self, for one's future. Having a place means planning, dealing with the world "out there," the world of "publicity." It means taking on the instrumental role that has so far been out of one's grasp. It means having the *choice* between living dependently and independently; having the *opportunity* to realize the promise. As one student of homeless women puts it,

The idea of being strong herself is frightening—less because it invites more punishment, which after all she is used to, than because it threatens the loss of whatever she has been getting, little as that may be. So she devalues whatever real strengths she may have in order to avoid even approaching this conflict. (Golden, 1986: 246)

The women who "break out" of the hostel circuit are known as "successes" to the staff. The sad reality is that they are the exceptions to the rule of chronic homelessness, "permanent transiency." One worker who had been involved with transient women for several years could count her "successes" on one hand.

Conclusions and Implications

Homelessness is not a problem unique to women; nor is it a problem unique to postindustrial, urbanized, patriarchal, capitalist society. Yet the current state of homelessness among women, the forms of social service response, and the ways in which women experience that response may, and indeed should, be understood in light of the wider context of women's experience and women's struggle in our society. For the homeless women tell us, through their common condition, much about the common condition of most women in our society, and certainly much about prevailing attitudes toward changing that condition.

Ideologically, homelessness among women is thought of as a condition to be corrected. Women who lack a "home" in the conventional sense of the word are deficient and are seen to need help. This is the view held by the state, media, public, and well-meaning imputational specialists. The nature of help has so far been in the form of emergency shelter. These hostels and drop-in centres, while providing desperately needed help, may also inadvertently serve to domesticate the homeless woman. The goal of "correcting" the condition must be carefully examined in light of the strategies employed for "helping."

Homelessness as Deficiency

The homeless woman is defined as deficient in two very fundamental ways. Homelessness entails lack of property and lack of family. Private property, the icon of capitalist society, is nowhere more evident than in home ownership. Home ownership is a pervasive indicator of success: when one buys a home, one "buys" citizenship. The person who lacks a home of her own must live somewhere: this is an assumption that few would question. People who earn incomes may be able to afford rental housing. People who do not may have no other choice but to live on the street.

"Family" is another rarely challenged bastion of capitalist and patriarchal society, primarily because, as an ideological institution, it is essential to the persistence of that society. The conventional notion of the family entails a fairly rigid structure: it is nuclear (involving spouses and their children) and patriarchal (male-dominated).

Together, property and family constitute a powerful ideological force that I have called the myth of home. This ideology is mythical because few "family arrangements" in fact correspond to it. Home can remain mythical because it is invisible: family is hidden behind the walls of the home. What we see, what we know, are images created and disseminated by the mass media, schools, and organized religion, of what the family "should be." These images keep most of us conforming unquestioningly most of the time, and feeling inadequate when our home life does not quite measure up. The ideology is forceful enough to produce a dependency among women on the male-dominated family unit, and to make it unthinkable for many women to aspire to be "independent."

The home embodies private property and patriarchy in the context of privacy. There has long been debate over the state's rights, duties, and obligations to citizens in terms of intervening in family affairs. This is because the family is the last outpost, the ultimate refuge from the state, from the formal forces of social control that regulate public places. In private, "a man is the king of his castle." In law and custom, women and children have long been considered chattels or slaves, the property of the home owner. This helps to explain the great reluctance with which the state has come to intervene in family violence. Within an ideology that holds the family as the goal of "normal living," the existence of the "pathological" family is systematically denied. Yet, state intervention in the form of state patriarchy has increased phenomenally during this century, and serves to further bolster the myth of home.

Homelessness among women is replete with ideological connotations. A woman without a home is first a woman without property (*read*: a woman without a man who has property), and second, she is a woman without family. A woman without family is a failure. She has failed to fulfil her role in life: that of wife and mother and purveyor of domestic bliss. If, as is frequently the case with homeless women, she has once occupied the role of wife and mother and does so no longer, she is regarded as being deficient, as somehow the source of the problem. It is irrelevant that the "domestic bliss" might have been abruptly shattered by the woman's choice to leave a violent or abusive living arrangement. Attributing deficiency to homeless women is both explicit and implicit in efforts to "help" them.

This tendency is clearly an example of "blaming the victim." Homeless women are seen to be in need of correction, in need of "rehabilitation" so that they will no longer be homeless but "homeful." But we must ask what this means. Remember the state that perpetrates the myth of home is the same state that defines homeless women as deficient. What they lack, and what they therefore must learn, is "domesticity."

Hostels as Reproducing Domesticity

While each individual hostel is unique in its design, emphasis, policies, and rules, in general the emergency hostel is designed to give the woman a temporary home until she has found a new one. Broadly speaking, we may identify three general types of women who seek shelter. First, there are women escaping violent, abusive or other emergency situations who have nowhere else to turn, and who are able to use the shelter temporarily until they have made arrangements for income and housing on their own. These are known to the staff as the "successes." Second, there are battered and abused women who are not able to "make it" on their own and who see returning to their spouses as their only viable route to "homefulness." Third, there are the chronically homeless who live on the street and in hostels. These are known to the staff as the "regulars." Hostels are not adequately equipped to help all three groups because these women present very different needs. Hostels tend to be under-funded, understaffed, and overcrowded. Length of stay is usually lim-ited to a few weeks—barely enough time for a woman to collect herself emotionally, let alone reconstruct her life. Privacy and autonomy are virtually impossible. Conflicts and violence often erupt between resi-dents. Such an environment is not always conducive to "helping," nor does it always offer a compelling alternative to "home."

The "successes" somehow manage, in spite of the system, to gather enough inner resources to break away from their dependency upon the family. Those who return to abusive situations do so for many reasons: guilt, "love", fear of being alone, fear of reprisal from their spouse, fear of poverty. Some will always go back, but others might be empowered to begin again if more realistic "options" for self-sufficiency, in the form of affordable housing, social support, and employment opportunities, were made available. The limited availability of these resources has the net effect of reproducing the cycle of women's dependency.

Finally, the women in the third group have become totally dependent upon the hostel system. The longer they are homeless, the less hope they seem to have to become "homeful". The hostel has come to *replace* home for them. Women who become dependent upon hostels learn that here they may exist, in perpetuity, without money or resources of any kind. The hostels reproduce traditional female roles by being modeled after homes and requiring women to do daily housekeeping chores, and by subjecting them to the rules and regulations of a larger structure that makes the decisions and has disciplinary power. In other words, they teach, foster, and reward domesticity.

Dependency is fostered among the chronically homeless because the hostels provide a safe place—no men allowed. They offer all the "com-forts of home"—with their ironic familiarity to the myth of home. In its efforts to "help" by providing shelter, the hostels have effectively repro-duced the conventional family relationships and displaced the role of the woman from being dependent upon the man to being dependent upon the provision of social services. This larger structure has taken on the role of the patriarch in their lives. The underlying condition of dependency is not challenged, for to challenge it would be to recognize that it is conceivable for women to be independent. Such a recognition threatens the very foundations of patriarchy and of capitalism.

Alternative Helping Strategies

What kind of help do homeless women need? While it has been stated above that different women have different needs, it can be safely said that all women, homeless or potentially homeless, need to be empowered. Help, through the emergency shelters, is vital and must not be done away with. But shelters are not enough. For the shelters, by making homeless women "homeful," make them invisible yet again.

Homefulness must come to mean control, autonomy, self-reliance. In most cases it is not possible to achieve these ends if women return out of desperation to destructive relationships, or if they become recidivists to the hostel circuit. In these cases, no serious opportunities are offered for women to break out of the polarization between expressive and instrumental role structures. Instead, like a boomerang, they keep going "home" to the familiar: they are continually redomesticated.

In the short run, the provision of affordable housing for the poor is absolutely crucial and should have high priority. This would relieve much of the source of the current crisis, and hopefully the trap of chronic homelessness and dependency could be averted by many women who find themselves needing emergency shelter.

In the long run, however, the patriarchal inclination to domesticate women must be challenged and done away with. Roles must be redefined so that it is acceptable and desirable for women to begin thinking of life on their own. Fundamental change in the institutions which support the existing patriarchal system, particularly the educational system and the kinship system, is required before roles may be redefined. This is a long-term project that one hopes will result in the abolition of many of the ways in which women and men suffer "learned helplessness" at the hands of a gendered division of labour. But the biggest hurdle that must be overcome is the reluctance of the state to relinquish control. For as long as social policy reflects the embedded ideology of the patriarchal state, then "help" will be no more than a "band-aid" applied to hide and perpetuate the problem.

Note

1. James E. Côté has observed that in this regard the hostel is remarkably similar to a "correctional centre." Minimal security correctional centres, for example, produce and enforce idle dependency. And while it is easy to "escape," few inmates have anywhere to go or anything to be gained by doing this.

Bibliography

Ambert, Anne-Marie, 1976. *Sex Structure* (2nd Ed.). Don Mills: Longman.

Anderson, Nels, 1923. *The Hobo: The Sociology of the Homeless Man*. Chicago: University of Chicago Press.

Armstrong, Pat, 1984. *Labour Pains: Women's Work in Crisis*. Toronto: Women's Press.

Bahr, Howard M., and Theodore Caplow, 1974. *Old Men Drunk and Sober*. New York: New York University Press.

Bahr, Howard M., and Gerald R. Garrett, 1976. *Women Alone: The Disaffiliation of Urban Females*. Lexington: Lexington Books.

Barrett, Michele, and Mary McIntosh, 1982. *The Anti-Social Family*. London: Verso.

Bem, Sandra L., and Daryl J. Bem, 1983. "Training the woman to know her place: The power of a nonconscious ideology." pp. 87-97 in H. Robboy and C. Clark (Eds.), *Social Interaction: Readings in Sociology*. New York: St. Martin's Press.

Bingham, Richard D., Roy E. Green, and Sammis B. White, 1987. *The Homeless in Contemporary Society*. Newbury Park: Sage.

Birch, Eugenie Ladner (Ed.), 1985. *The Unsheltered Woman: Women and Housing in the 80's*. New Brunswick, N. J.: Center for Urban Policy Research.

Black, Henry Campbell, 1979. *Black's Law Dictionary*. St. Paul, Minn.: West Publishing.

Burstyn, Varda, and Dorothy E. Smith, 1985. *Women, Class, Family and the State*. Toronto: Garamond.

Chambliss, William, 1964. "A sociological analysis of the law of vagrancy," *Social Problems* 12:67-77.

Chesler, Phyllis, 1972. *Women and Madness*. New York: Avon.

Chodorow, Nancy, 1978. *The Reproduction of Mothering*. Berkeley: University of California Press.

Cole, Susan G., 1982. "Home sweet home?" pp. 55-67 in M. Fitzgerald, C. Guberman and M. Wolfe (eds.), *Still Ain't Satisfied! Canadian Feminism Today*. Toronto: The Women's Press.

Côté, James E., and Charles Levine, 1987. "A formulation of Erikson's theory of ego identity formation," *Developmental Review* 7:273-325.

Cuff, John Haslett, 1981. "Life in the street," *Globe and Mail*, August 1, 1981: F2.

Dickinson, James, and Bob Russell, 1986. *Family, Economy and State: The Social Reproduction Process Under Capitalism*. Toronto: Garamond.

Donzelot, Jacques, 1979. *The Policing of Families*. New York: Pantheon.

Ehrenreich, Barbara, and Deirdre English, 1978. *For Her Own Good: 150 Years of the Experts' Advice to Women*. New York: Anchor.

Eichler, Margrit, 1983. *Families in Canada Today*. Toronto: Gage.

Fairbairns, Zoe, 1985. "The cohabitation rule—Why it makes sense," pp. 63-74 in C. Ungerson (ed.), *Women and Social Policy: A Reader*. London: Macmillan.

Garfinkel, Harold, 1956. "Conditions of successful degradation ceremonies," *American Journal of Sociology* 61:420-424.

Gitlin, Todd, 1979. "Prime time ideology: The hegemonic process in television entertainment," *Social Problems* 26(3):251-266.

Glaser, Barney G., and Anselm L. Strauss, 1967. *The Discovery of Grounded Theory: Strategies for Qualitative Research*. Chicago: Aldine.

Goffman, Erving, 1959. *The Presentation of Self in Everyday Life*. New York: Anchor.

1961. Asylums: *Essays on the Social Situation of Mental Patients and Other Inmates*. New York: Anchor.

1963a. *Behavior in Public Places: Notes on the Social Organization of Gatherings*. New York: Free Press.

1963b. *Stigma: Notes on the Management of Spoiled Identity*. Englewood Cliffs, N. J.: Prentice-Hall.

1971. *Relations in Public: Microstudies of the Public Order*. New York: Harper Colophon. Golden, Stephanie, 1979. "The transforming tree: Finding our roots in the homeless women," *Conditions* 4 (Winter): 82-95.

1986. "Daddy's good girls: Homeless women and 'mental illness'," pp. 235-247 in R. Lefkowitz and A. Withorn (eds.), *For Crying Out Loud: Women and Poverty in the United States*. New York: Pilgrim Press.

Harman, Lesley D., 1985. "Acceptable deviance as social control: The cases of fashion and slang," *Deviant Behavior* 6: 1-15.

1987a. *The Modern Stranger: On Language and Membership.* Berlin: Mouton de Gruyter.

1987b. "The creation of the 'bag lady': Rethinking home for homeless women," *Human Affairs* 12:58-86.

1988. "Public and private: Myths and the regulation of domestic life in Canadian society," *Journal of Canadian Studies* 23(3): 160-170.

Hayden, Dolores, 1981. *The Grand Domestic Revolution.* Cambridge: M. I. T. Press.

Hope, Marjorie, and James Young, 1986. *The Faces of Homelessness.* Lexington: Lexington Books.

Hughes, Everett, 1945. "Dilemmas and contradictions of status," *American Journal of Sociology* 50: 353-359.

Krotz, Larry, 1980. *Urban Indians: The Strangers in Canada's Cities.* Edmonton: Hurtig.

Lasch, Christopher, 1977. *Haven in a Heartless World.* New York: Basic.

Laws, Judith Long, 1979. *The Second X: Sex Role and Social Role.* New York: Elsevier.

Lefkowitz, Rochelle, and Ann Withorn (eds.), 1986. *For Crying Out Loud: Women and Poverty in the United States.* New York: Pilgrim.

Lofland, John, 1969. *Deviance and Identity.* Englewood Cliffs, N.J.: Prentice-Hall.

Luxton, Meg, 1986. "Two hands for the clock: Changing patterns in the gendered division of labour in the home," pp. 17-36 in M. Luxton and H. Rosenberg, *Through the Kitchen Window: The Politics of Home and Family.* Toronto: Garamond.

Luxton, Meg, and Harriet Rosenberg, 1986. *Through the Kitchen Window: The Politics of Home and Family.* Toronto: Garamond.

MacLeod, Linda, 1980. *Wife Battering in Canada: The Vicious Circle.* Ottawa: Ministry of Supply and Services Canada.

1987. *Battered But Not Beaten: Preventing Wife Battering in Canada.* Ottawa: Canadian Advisory Council on the Status of Women.

Martin, Del, 1977. *Battered Wives.* New York: Pocket Books.

McClain, Janet, with Cassie Doyle, 1984. *Women and Housing: Changing Needs and the Failure of Policy.* Ottawa: Canadian Council on Social Development.

Merton, Robert K., 1968. *Social Theory and Social Structure.* Glencoe, Ill: Free Press.

O'Brien, Mary, 1981. *The Politics of Reproduction*. London: Routledge and Kegan Paul.

Olson, Laura Katz, 1985. "Older women: Longevity, dependency, and public policy," pp. 157-175 in Virginia Sapiro (ed.), *Women, Biology, and Public Policy*. Beverly Hills: Sage.

Packard, Vance, 1972. *A Nation of Strangers*. New York: Pocket Books.

Park, Robert E., and Ernest W. Burgess, 1925. *The City*. Chicago: University of Chicago Press.

Parsons, Talcott, and Robert F. Bales, 1955. *Family, Socialization and Interaction Process*. New York: Free Press.

Rosenberg, Harriet, 1986. "The home is the workplace," pp. 37-61 in M. Luxton and H. Rosenberg, *Through the Kitchen Window: The Politics of Home and Family*. Toronto: Garamond.

Ross, Aileen, 1982. *The Lost and the Lonely: Homeless Women in Montreal*. Montreal: The Canadian Human Rights Foundation.

Rousseau, Ann Marie, 1981. *Shopping Bag Ladies: Homeless Women Speak About their Lives*. New York: Pilgrim.

Rubington, Earl, 1981. "Variations in bottle-gang controls," pp. 360-8 in E. Rubington and M.S. Weinberg (eds.), *Deviance: The Interactionist Perspective* (4th Ed.). New York: Macmillan.Sampson, Harold, Sheldon L. Messinger, and Robert D. Towne, 1962. "Family processes and becoming a mental patient," *American Journal of Sociology* 68: 88-96.

Sapiro, Virginia, 1985. "Biology and women's policy: A view from the Social Sciences," pp. 41-64 in Virginia Sapiro (ed.), *Women, Biology, and Public Policy*. Beverly Hills: Sage.

Schur, Edwin M., 1984. *Labeling Women Deviant: Gender, Stigma, and Social Control*. New York: Random House.

Schutz, Alfred, 1944. "The stranger: An essay in social psychology," *American Journal of Sociology* 49: 499-507.

Shaffir, William B., Robert A. Stebbins, and Allan Turowetz (eds), 1980. *Fieldwork Experience: Qualitative Approaches to Social Research*. New York: St. Martin's Press.

Smith, Dorothy E., 1985. "Women, class and family," pp. 1-44 in V. Burstyn and D.E. Smith, *Women, Class, Family and the State*. Toronto: Garamond.

Spradley, James P., 1979. *The Ethnographic Interview*. New York: Holt, Rinehart and Winston.

—— 1980. *Participant Observation*. New York: Holt, Rinehart and Winston.

Sullivan, Patricia A., and Shirley P. Damrosch, 1987. "Homeless women and children," pp. 82-98 in Richard D. Bingham, Roy E. Green, and Sammis B. White (Eds.), *The Homeless in Contemporary Society*. Beverly Hills: Sage.

Szasz, Thomas, 1974. *The Myth of Mental Illness*. New York: Harper and Row.

Taylor, Paul, 1986. "Chose own lifestyle, inquest on woman told," *Globe and Mail*, Feb. 13, 1986, p. A1.

Thompson, Judy and R. Gilby, 1980. "Correlates of domestic violence and the role of police agencies," pp. 298-306 in R.A. Silverman and J.J. Teevan (eds.), *Crime in Canadian Society* (2nd. Ed.). Toronto: Butterworths.

Thrasher, Anthony A., 1976. *Thrasher: Skid Row Eskimo*. Toronto: Griffin House.

Tierney, Kathleen J., 1982. "The battered women movement and the creation of the wife beating problem," *Social Problems* 29(3): 207-220.

Tindale, Joseph, 1977. "The management of self among old men of skid row," *Essence* 2(1): 49-58.

Ungerson, Clare (Ed.), 1985. *Women and Social Policy: A Reader*. London: Macmillan.

Ursel, Jane, 1986. "The state and the maintenance of patriarchy: A case study of family, labour and welfare legislation in Canada," pp. 150-191 in J. Dickinson & B. Russell (eds.), *Family, Economy and State: The Social Reproduction Process under Capitalism*. Toronto: Garamond.

Wallace, Samuel E., 1968. "The road to skid row," *Social Problems* 16(1): 96-102.

Warren, Carol E., 1988. *Gender Issues in Field Research*. Beverly Hills: Sage.

Watson, Sophie, with Helen Austerberry, 1986. *Housing and Homelessness: A Feminist Perspective*. London: Routledge and Kegan Paul.

Weitz, Shirley, 1979. *Sex Roles*. New York: Oxford University Press.

Wilson, Elizabeth, 1977. *Women and the Welfare State*. London: Tavistock.

Wineman, Steven, 1984. *The Politics of Human Services: Radical Alternatives to the Welfare State*. Montreal: Black Rose Books.

Wiseman, Jacqueline P., 1970. *Stations of the Lost: The Treatment of Skid Row Alcoholics*. Englewood Cliffs, N.J.: Prentice-Hall.

Wright, Rolland H., 1971. "The stranger mentality and the culture of poverty," pp. 315-337 in E. Leacock (ed.), *The Culture of Poverty*. New York: Simon and Schuster.

Zaretsky, Eli, 1976. *Capitalism, The Family, and Personal Life*. New York: Harper Torchbooks.

About the Author

Lesley D. Harman was born in Canada in 1956 and received her Ph.D. in Sociology from York University in 1983. She is the author of *The Modern Stranger: On Language and Membership*, as well as several articles in women's studies, the sociology of deviance, and social theory. She is currently living in London, Ontario, where she teaches in the Department of Sociology at King's College, The University of Western Ontario.